# 4 0 0 0
## MONOGRAMS

MONOGRAMME
MONOGRAMMES
MONOGRAMMI
MONOGRAMAS

# 4000
## MONOGRAMS

MONOGRAMME
MONOGRAMMES
MONOGRAMMI
MONOGRAMAS

THE PEPIN PRESS

Copyright for this edition © 1998 The Pepin Press B/v
Copyright introduction '4000 Monograms' © 1998 The Pepin Press B/v

First published in 1998 by The Pepin Press

Edited and produced by Dorine van den Beukel

ISBN 90 5496 045 0

The Pepin Press
POB 10349 • 1001 EH Amsterdam • The Netherlands
Tel (+) 31 20 4202021 • Fax (+) 31 20 4201152 • E-Mail pepin@euronet.nl

Printed in Singapore

# 4000 Monograms

A monogram is a character consisting of two or more interwoven letters or ciphers, intended as an abbreviation, mostly of a name. The word *monogram* is derived from the Greek *monos* 'single' and *gramma* 'letter'. Probably one of the most well-known examples is that formed by the letters *chi* and *rho*, the first letters of the Greek *Christos*, Christ.

In Greek and Roman times, the monograms of heads of state were used on coins, medals, and monuments. Charlemagne was the first ruler to use his monogram as a signature on documents. Frankish, French and German sovereigns continued this practice until well into the 13th century. Later, monograms were used as trademarks by merchants who were not entitled to display a coat of arms. Generally, these monograms consisted of the owner's initials with a private device. Early printers used monograms on their title pages, and artists used them for signing their engravings and paintings.

Nowadays, monograms are mostly used as trademarks, or as a mark of ownership, for instance on handkerchiefs or ex libris book-plates.

# 4000 Monogramme

Ein Monogramm ist ein Zeichen von zwei oder mehr miteinander verbundenen Buchstaben, das meist zur Abkürzung eines Names verwendet wird. Das Wort "Monogramm" kommt aus dem griechischen *Monos* (Einzahl) und *Gramma* (Buchstabe). Eines der wohl berühmtesten Monogramme setzt sich aus den Buchstaben *Chi* und *Rho* zusammen, den ersten beiden Buchstaben des griechischen Wortes *Christos*.

In der griechischen und römischen Antike wurden Monogramme auf Münzen, Medaillen und Monumenten angebracht. Karl der Grosse war der erste Herrscher, der sein Monogramm als Unterschrift auf Dokumente setzte. Dieser Brauch wurde von fränkischen, französischen und deutschen Fürsten bis in das 13. Jahrhundert fortgesetzt. Später wurden Monogramme von Kaufleuten, die kein Wappen tragen durften, als Handelszeichen verwendet. Die ersten Drucker bildeten Monogramme auf ihren Titelseiten ab, und Künstler benutzten sie als Unterschrift für ihre Holzschnitte und Bilder.

Heutzutage werden Monogramme vor allem als *Trademarks* (Markenzeichen) oder als Kennzeichnung für Eigentum gebraucht, wie zum Beispiel auf Taschentüchern oder auf Ex Libris.

# 4000 Monogrammes

Un monogramme est un charactère constitué de plusieurs lettres ou chiffres entrelacés, destinés à former une abbréviation; d'un nom principalement. Le mot *monogramme* est dérivé du grec *monos* 'unique' et *gramma* 'lettre'. Probablement l'un des examples de monogrammes le plus fameux est celui formé par les lettres *chi* et *rho*, premières lettres du grec *Christos*, Christ.

Aux temps Gréco-romains, des monogrammes de souverains apparurent sur les pièces de monnaie, médailles et monuments. Charlemagne fut le premier souverain à se servir de son monogramme pour signer des documents. Les souverains Francs, Français et Allemands perpétuèrent cette pratique jusqu'à une bonne partie du treizième siècle. Plus tard, les monogrammes servirent de marques de fabrication pour les marchands n'étant pas habilités à arborer un blason. Généralement, ces monogrammes représentaient les initiales du propriétaire avec un emblème personnel. Les premiers imprimeurs utilisèrent les monogrammes sur leur pages de titre et les artistes pour signer leurs gravures ou leurs peintures.

De nos jours, les monogrammes constituent des marques de fabrication ou de propriété en general; comme par example sur des mouchoirs ou des ex-libris.

# 4000 Monogrammi

Il monogramma è un segno formato dall'intreccio di due o più lettere dell'alfabeto, ed è inteso come abbreviazione, per lo più di un nome proprio. La parola *monogramma* deriva dalle parole greche *monos* (singolo) e *gramma* (lettera). Probabilmente uno dei più noti monogrammi è quello formato dalle lettere greche *chi* e *ro*, le prime due del nome di Cristo in greco: *Christos.*

Nel mondo antico greco-romano si ponevano monogrammi di sovrani sulle monete, sulle medaglie e sui monumenti. Carlo Magno fu il primo sovrano a firmare documenti con il proprio monogramma, imitato dai successivi sovrani franchi, francesi e tedeschi fino al Duecento addentrato. Poi i monogrammi si cominciarono a usare come marchi commerciali di mercanti, che non avevano il diritto di portare un blasone. Generalmente questi monogrammi erano formati dalle iniziali del proprietario con un motto personale. I primi stampatori apponevano monogrammi sui frontespizi dei libri e gli artisti li usavano per firmare incisioni e dipinti.

Oggigiorno i monogrammi si usano generalmente come marchi di fabbrica o per identificare il proprietario, per esempio sui fazzoletti e negli ex libris.

# 4000 Monogramas

Un monograma es un carácter que consiste en dos o más letras o cifras entrelazadas a modo de abreviatura, generalmente de un nombre. La palabra *monograma* proviene del griego *monos* "única" y *gramma* "letra".

Probablemente, uno de los ejemplos más conocidos sea el formado por las letras *chi* y *rho*, las dos primeras de la palabra *Christos*, en griego Cristo. En los imperios griego y romano se utilizaron monogramas de los gobernantes en las monedas, medallas y monumentos. Carlomagno fue el primer gobernante que utilizó su monograma para firmar los documentos. Numerosos soberanos francos, franceses y alemanes siguieron esta costumbre hasta bien entrado el siglo XIII. Más tarde, los mercaderes que no estaban autorizados a representar un escudo de armas utilizaron monogramas como marcas comerciales. Normalmente, tales monogramas consistían en las iniciales de su propietario con algún emblema personal. Los primeros impresores utilizaron monogramas en las portadas y los artistas firmaron con ellos sus cuadros y grabados.

Hoy en día, el uso de los monogramas se limita a las marcas comerciales y como marca de propiedad en ex libris y pañuelos, por ejemplo.

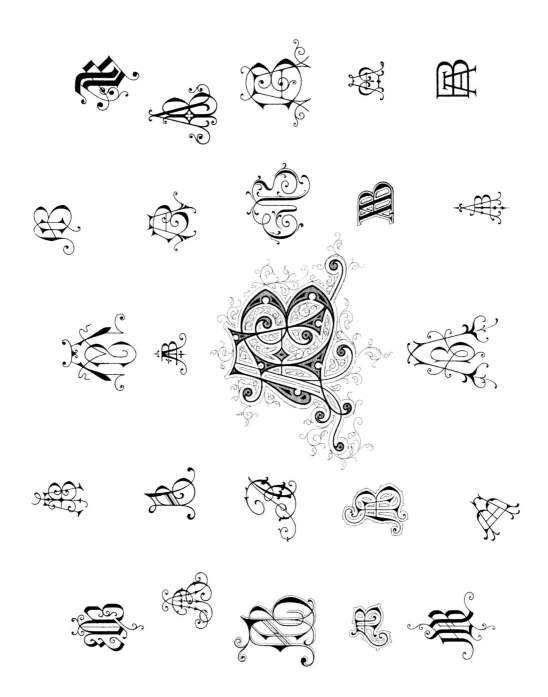

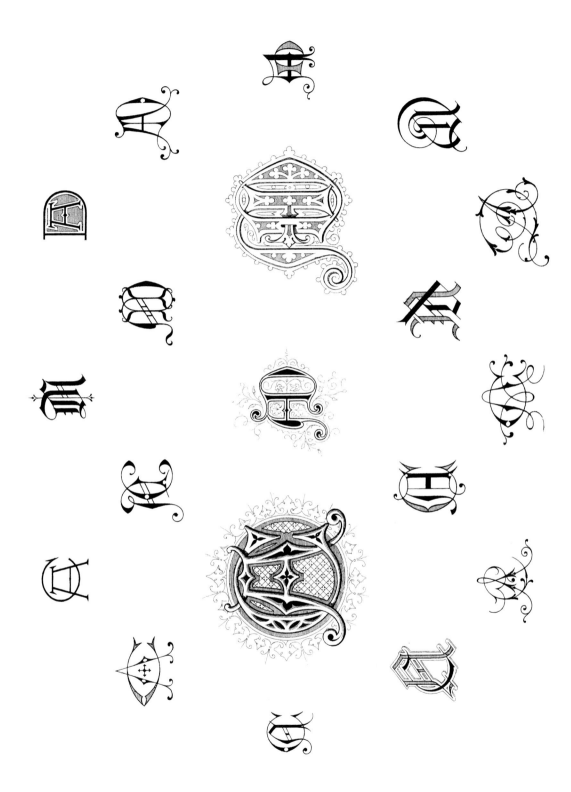

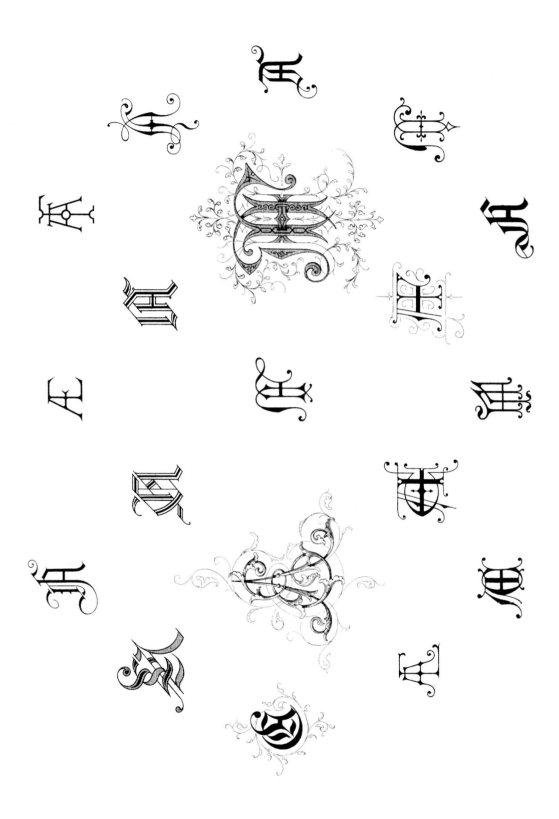

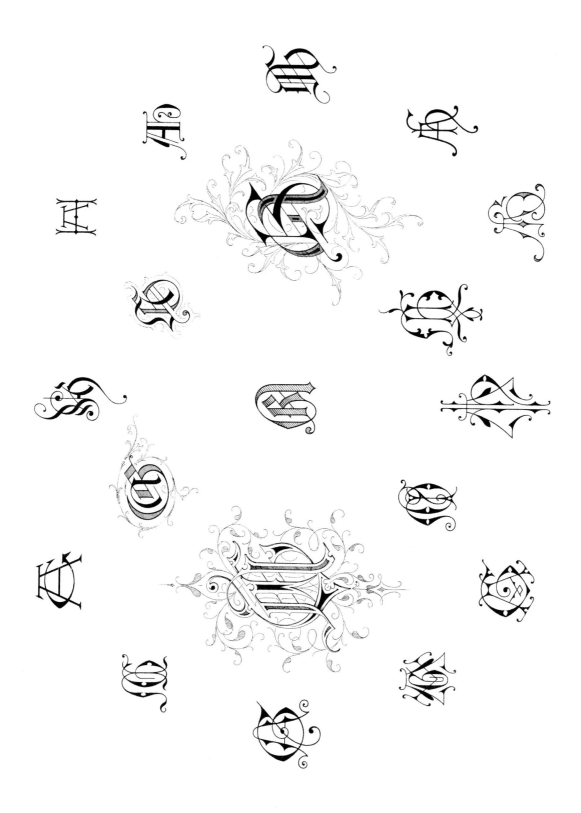

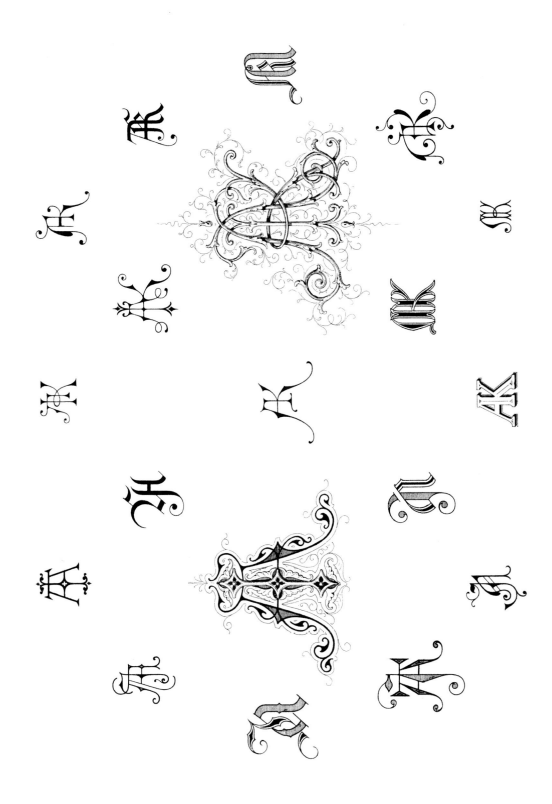

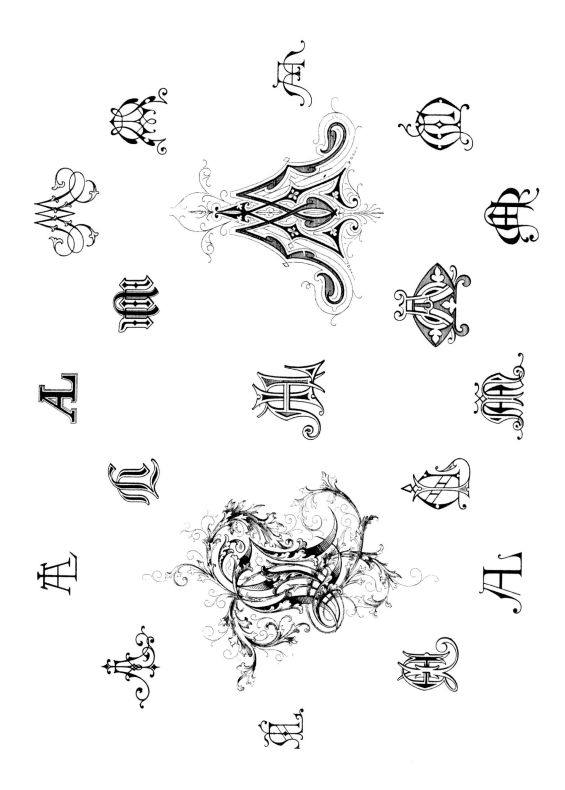

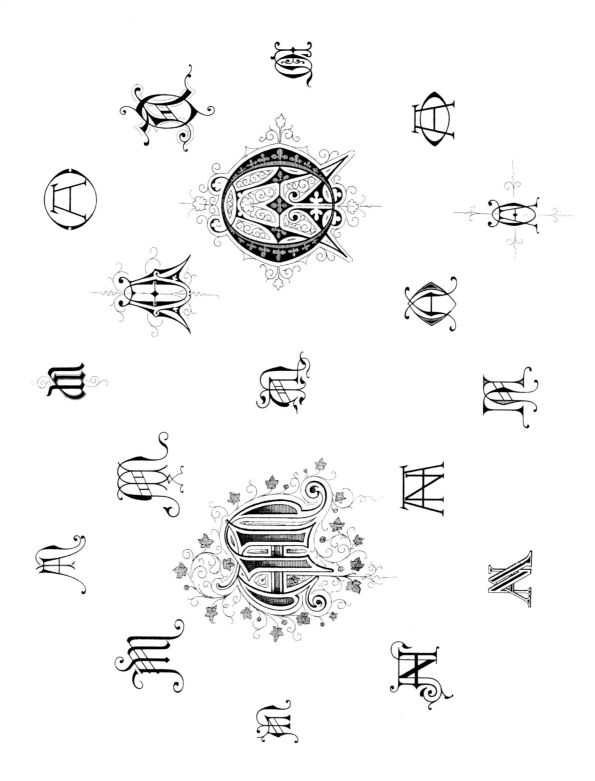

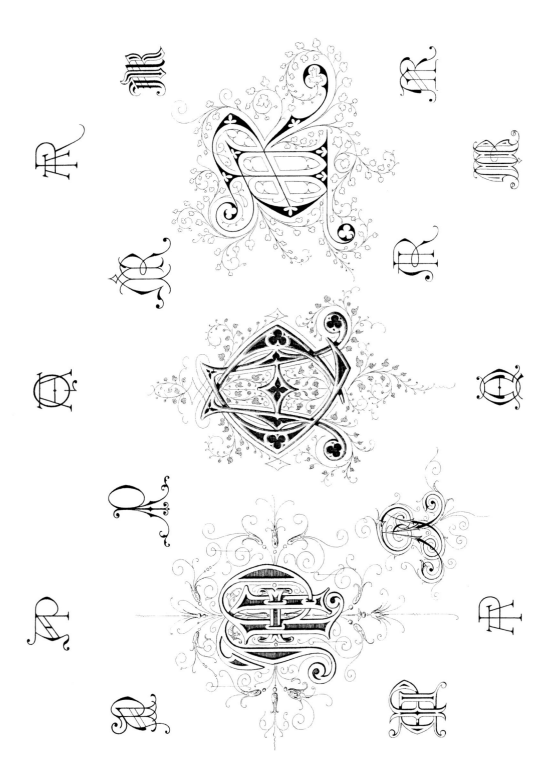

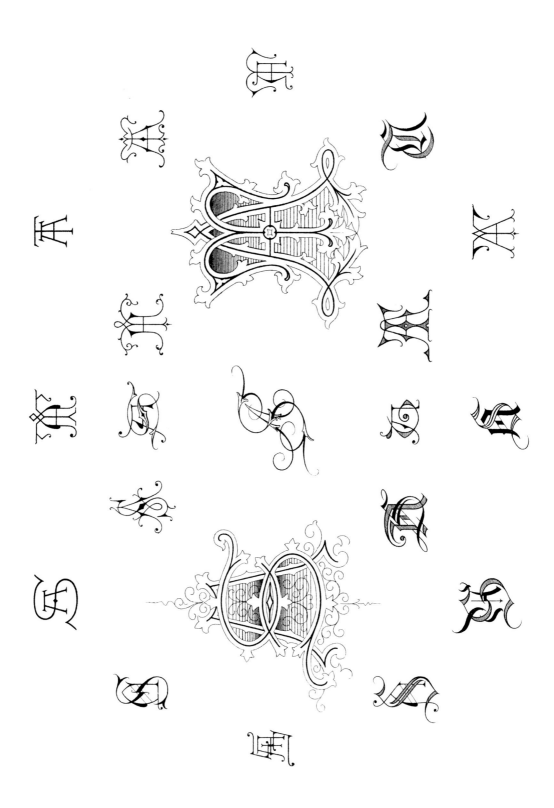

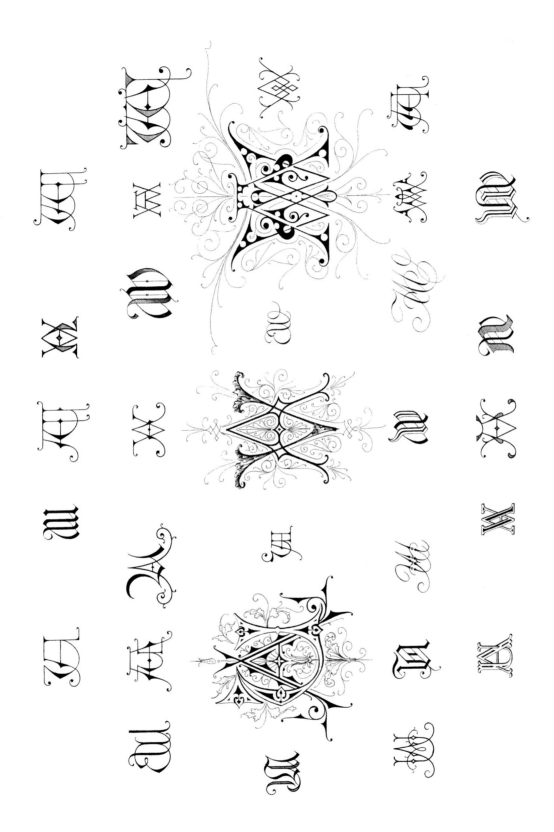

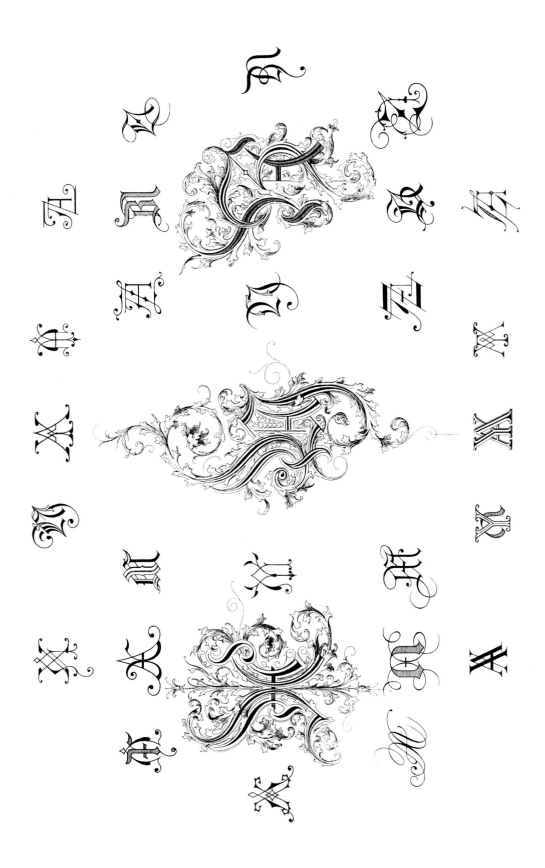

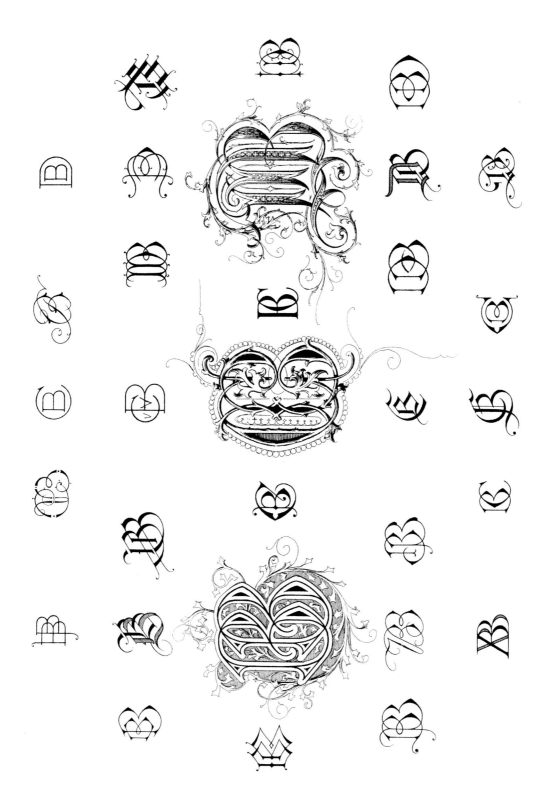

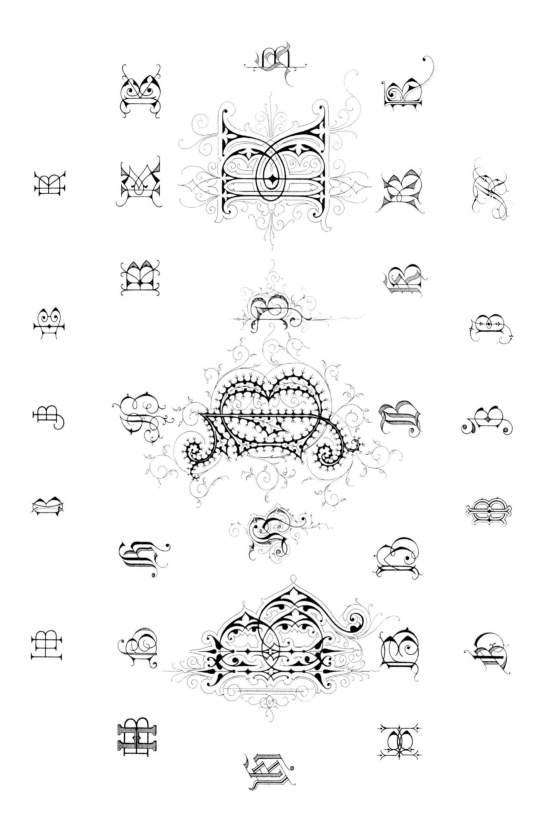

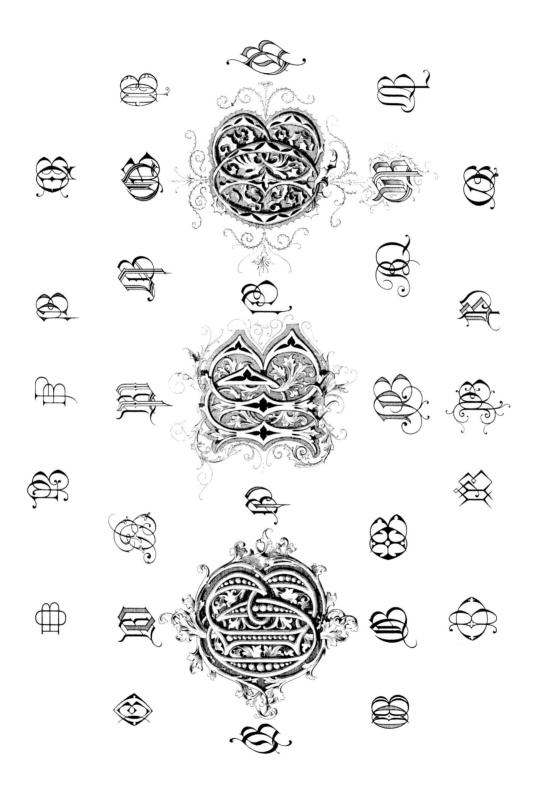

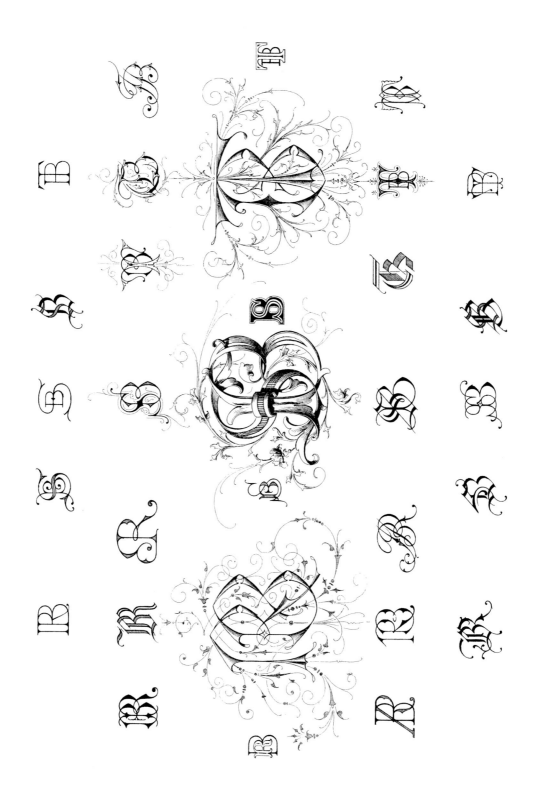

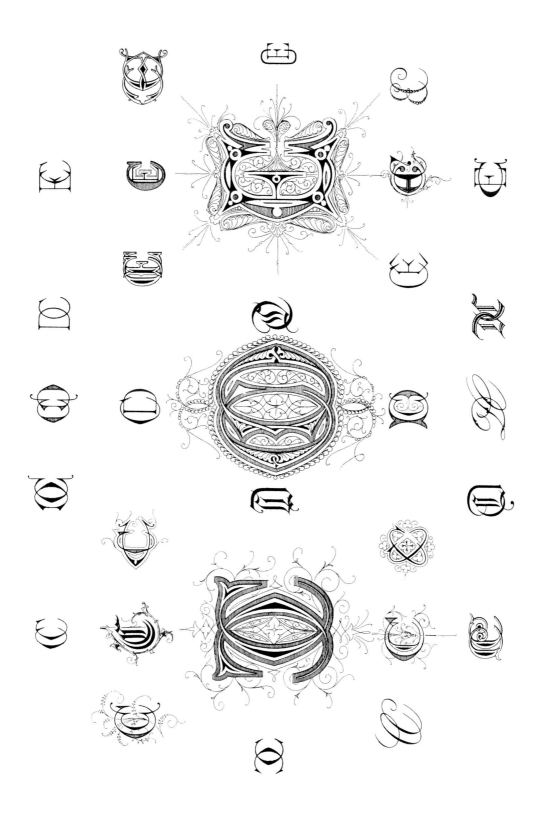

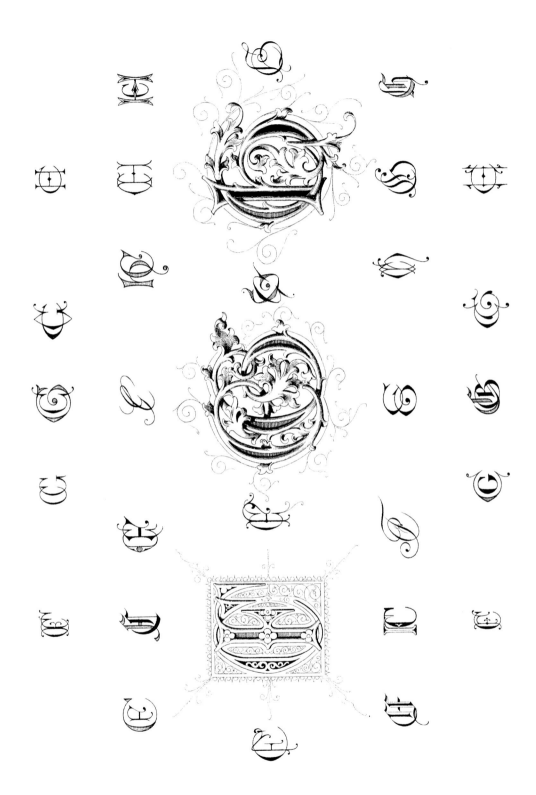

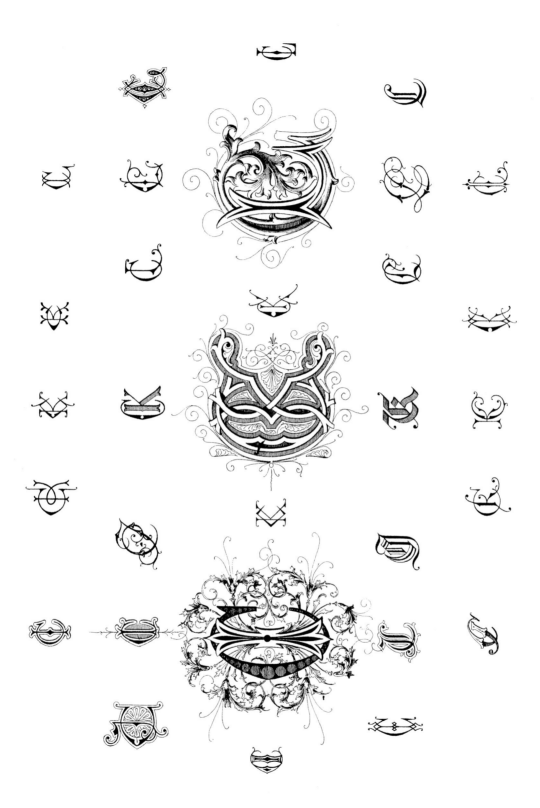

33

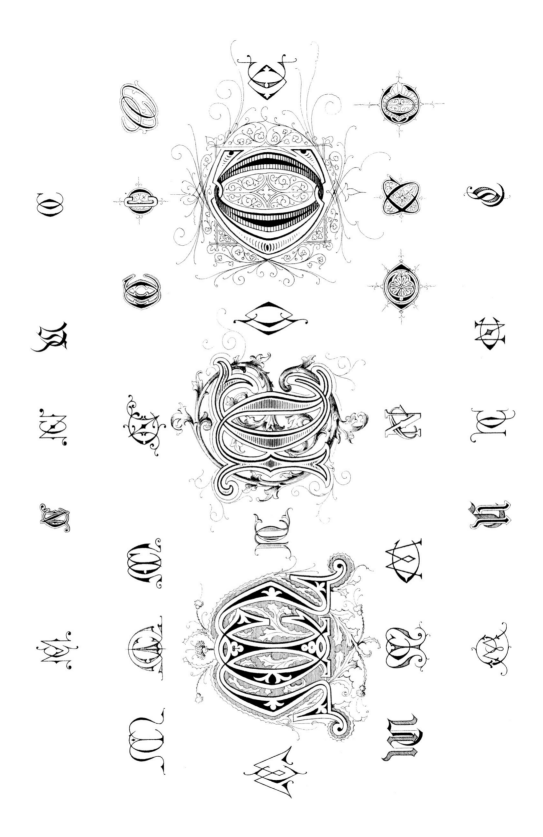

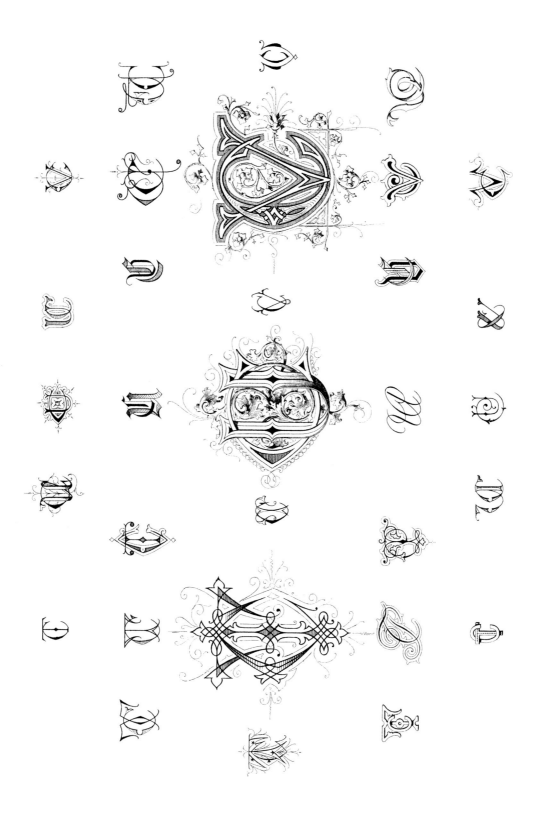

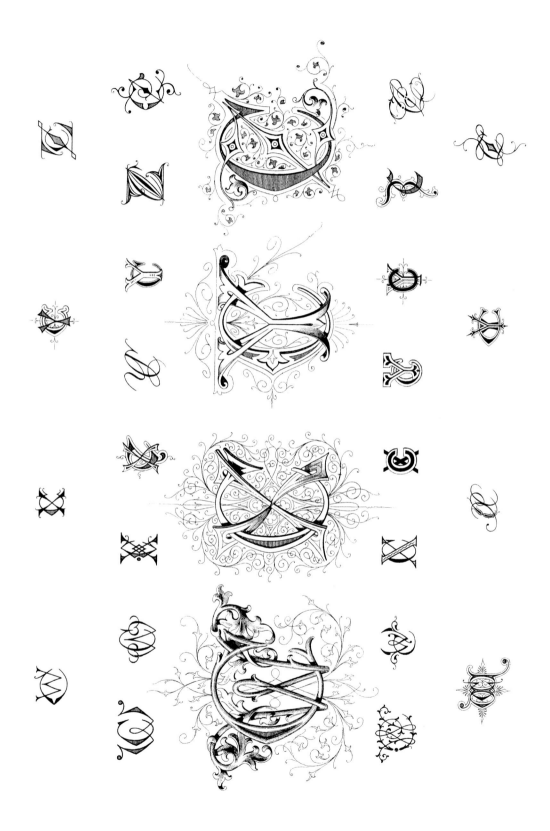

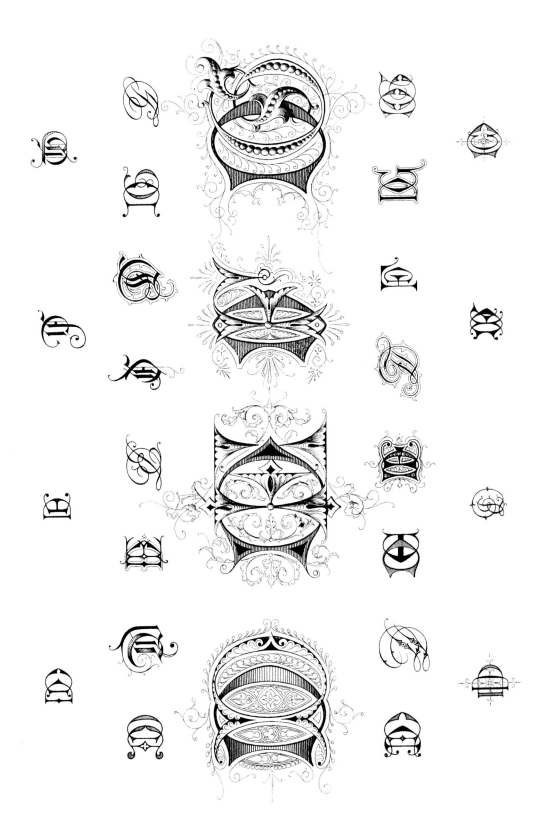

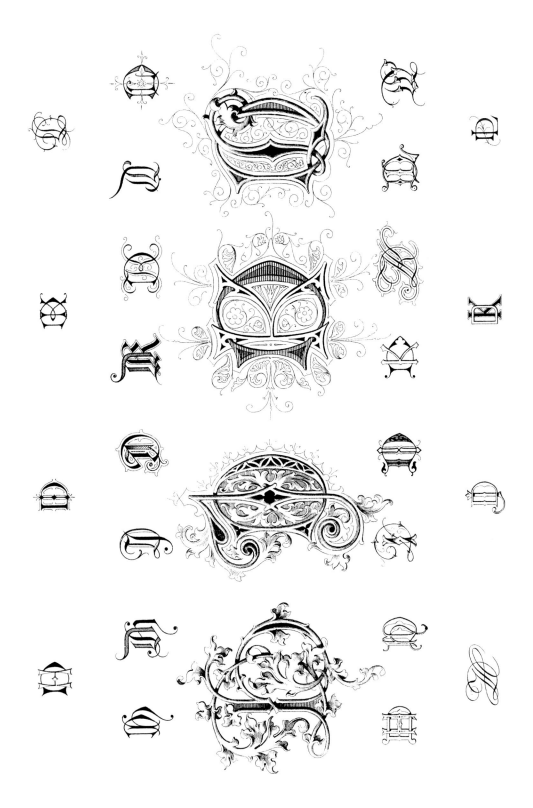

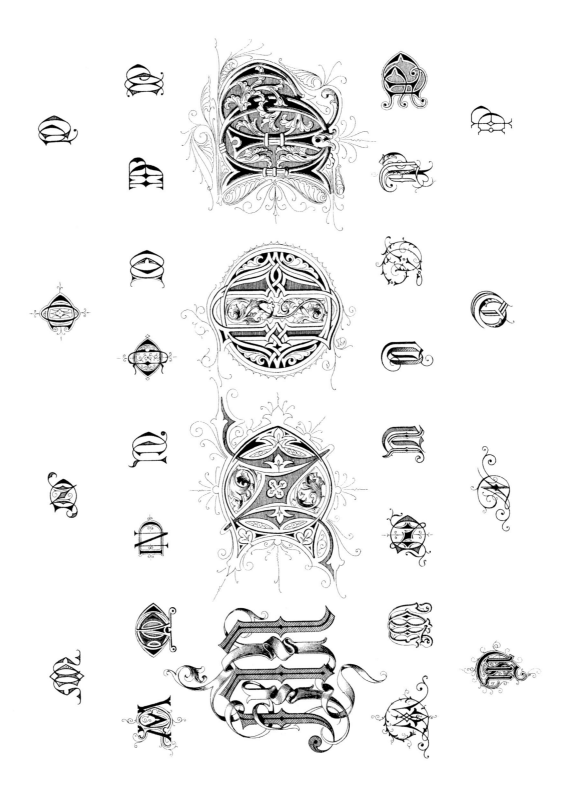

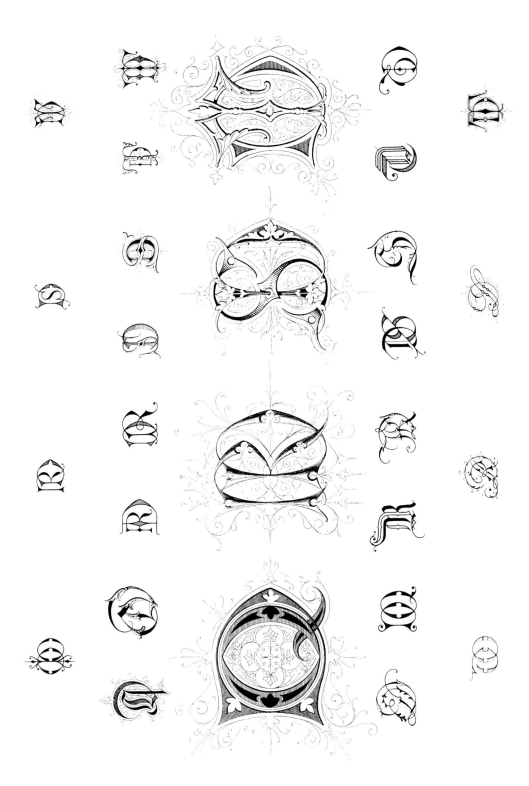

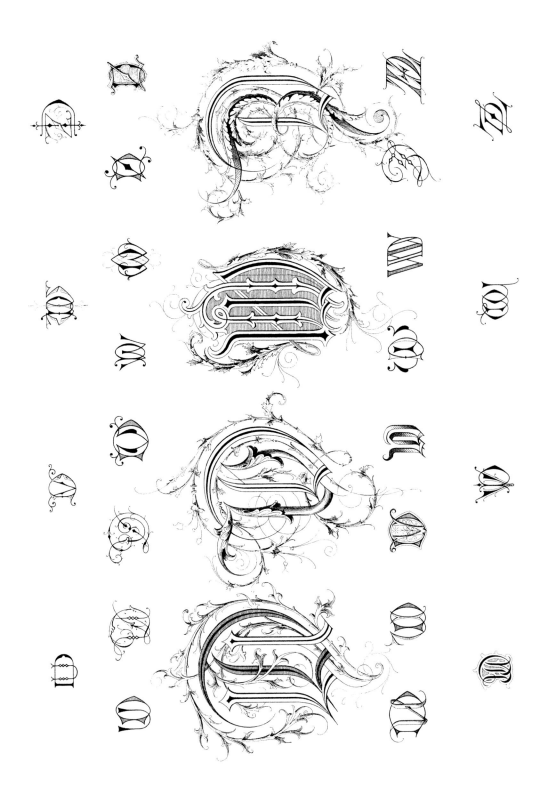

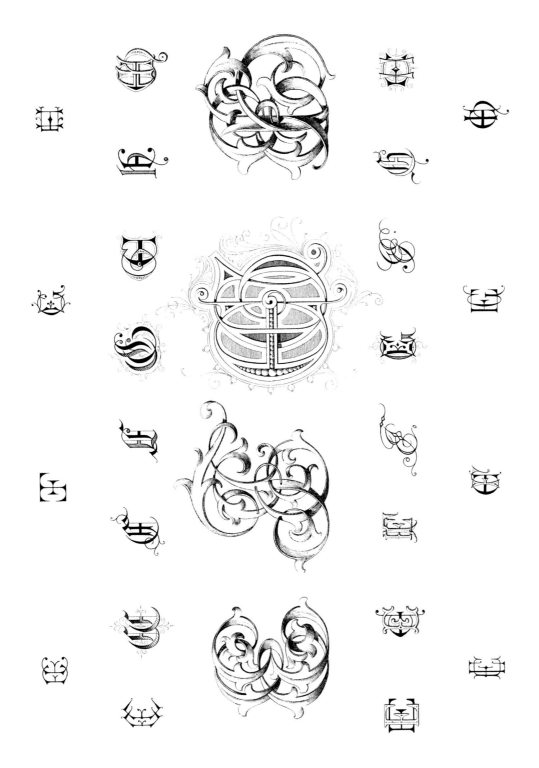

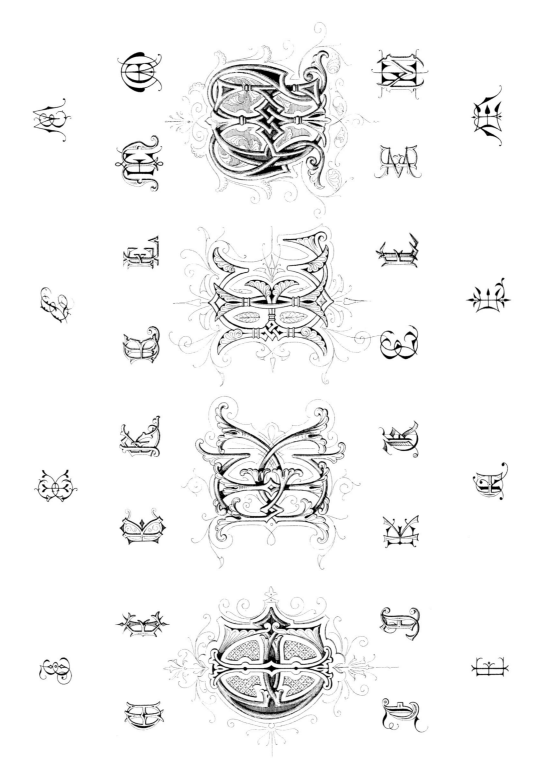

44

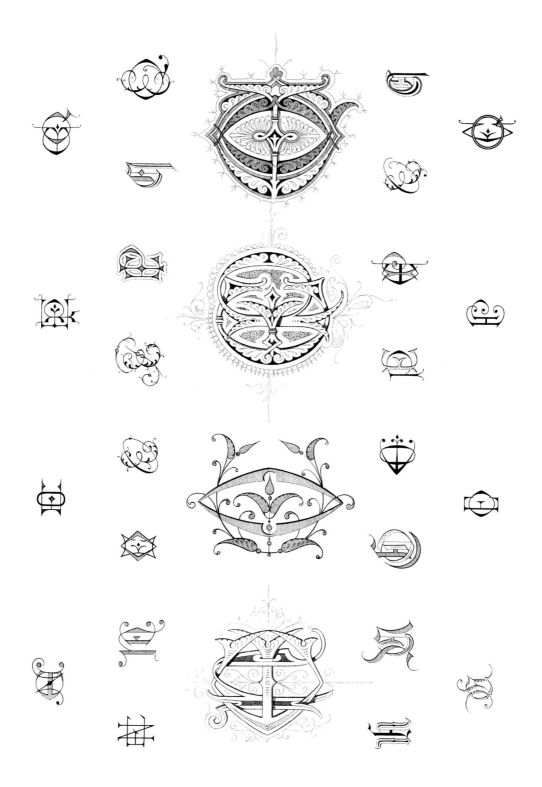

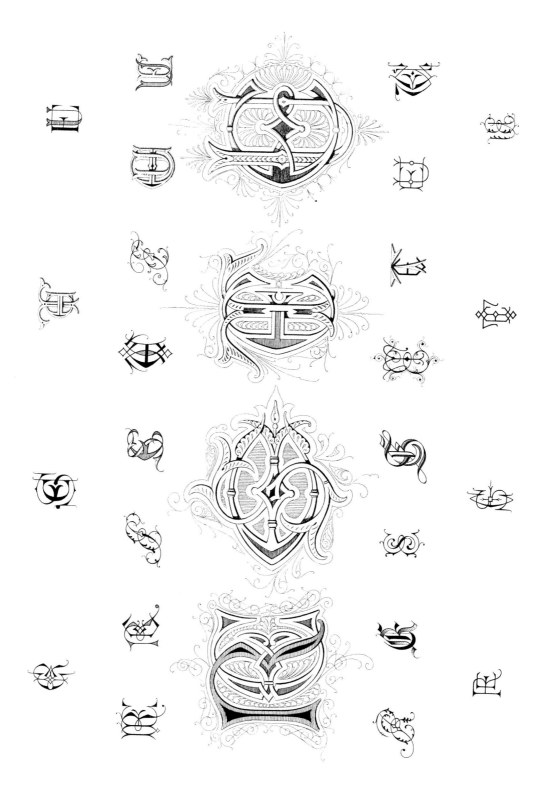

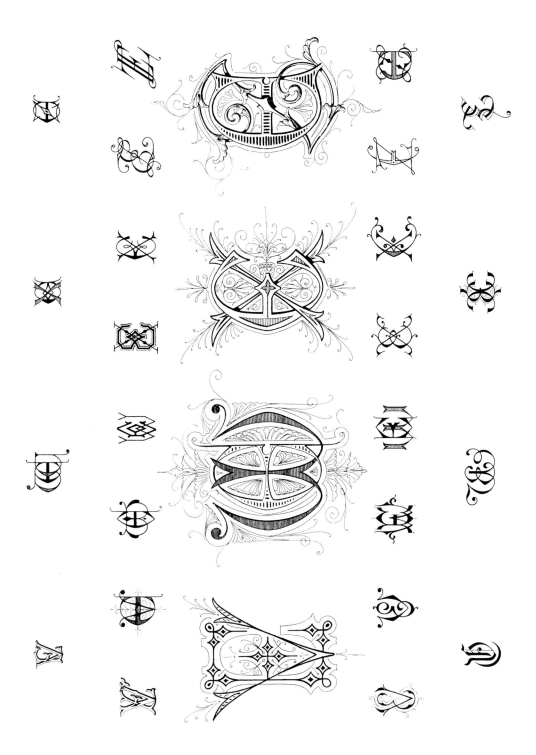

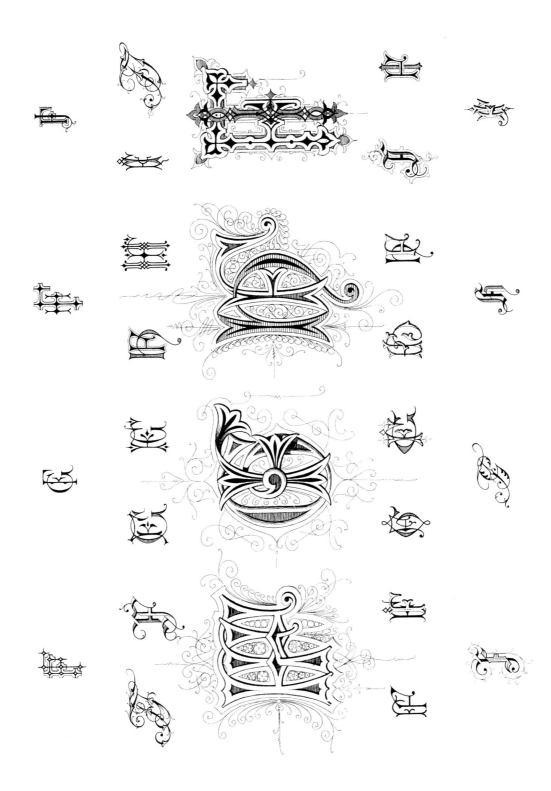

48

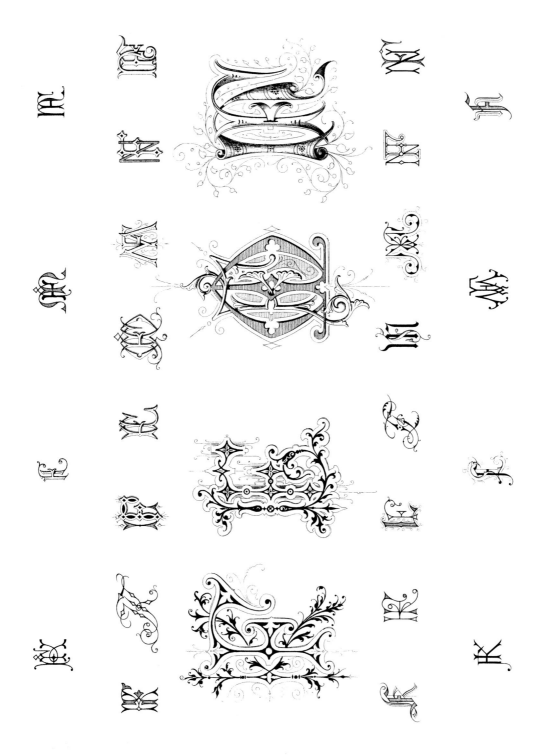

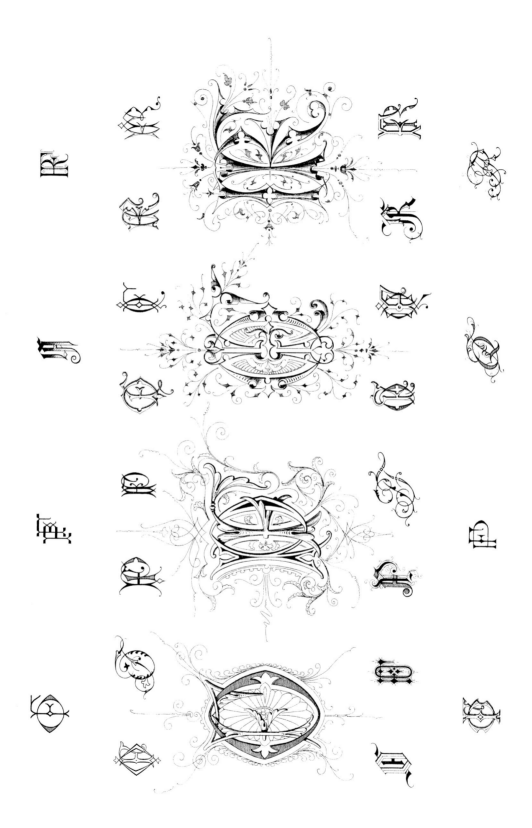

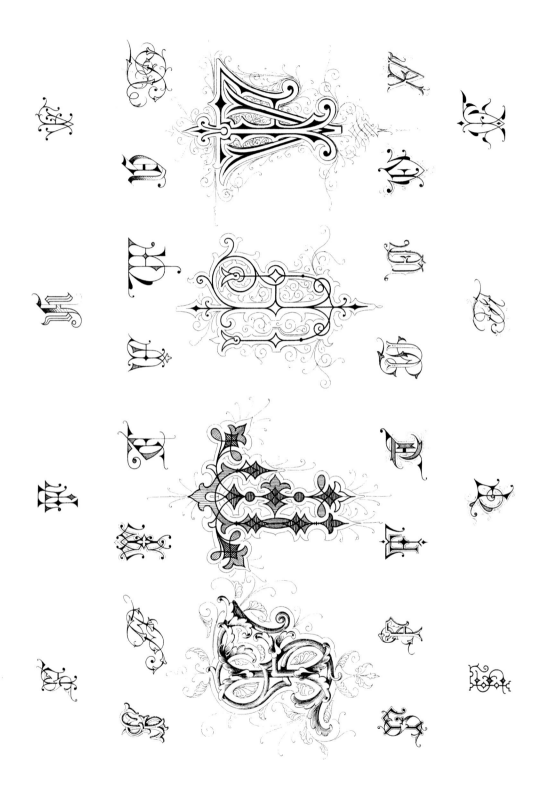

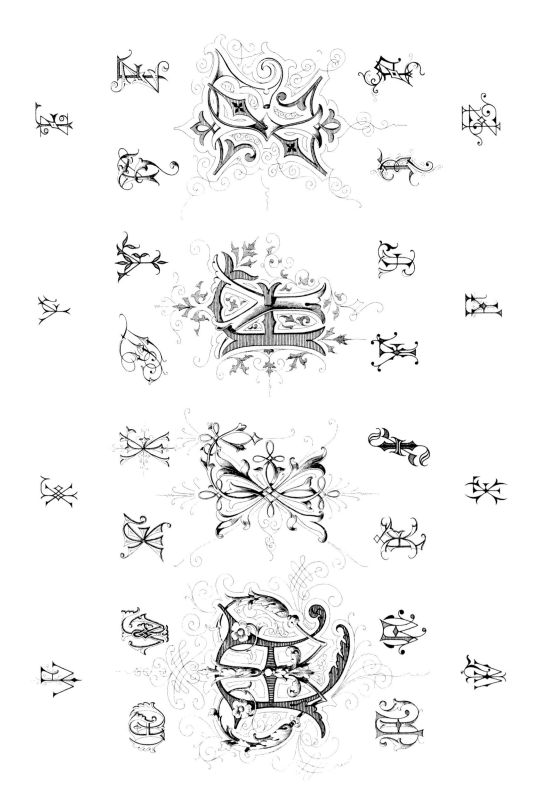

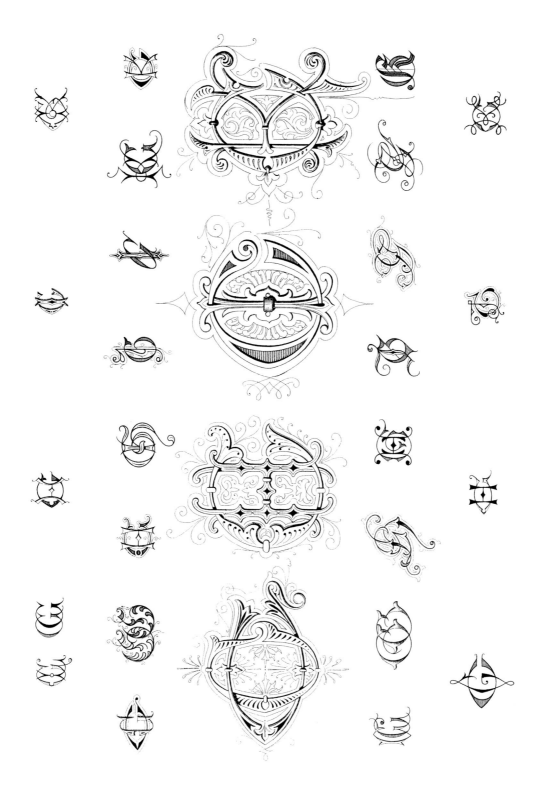

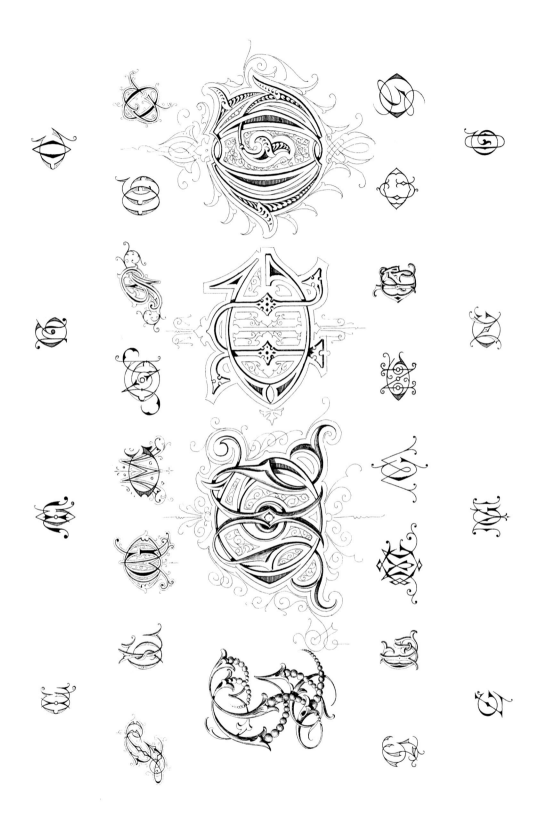

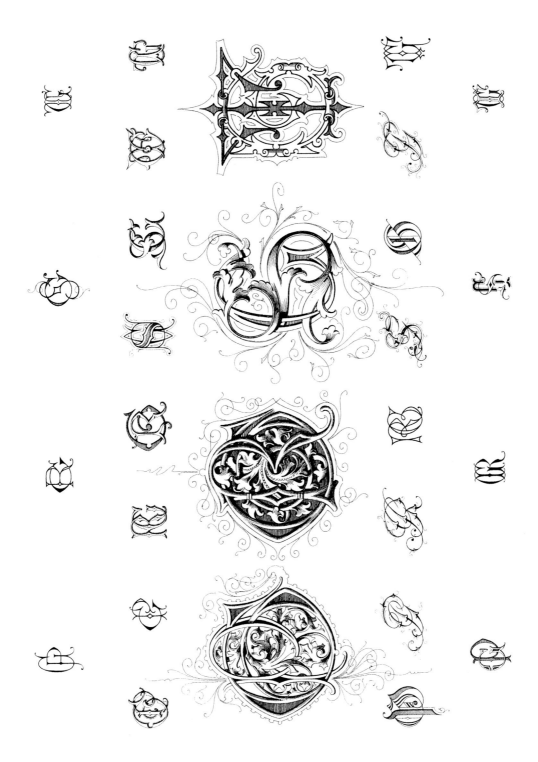

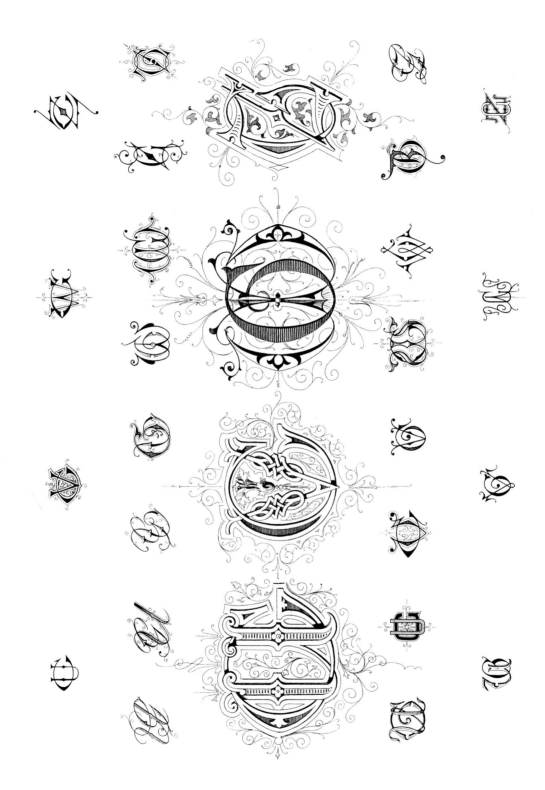

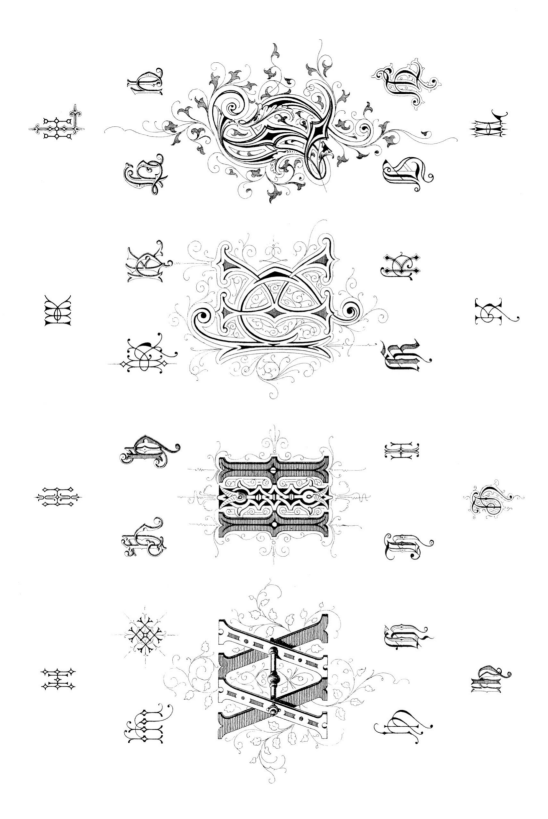

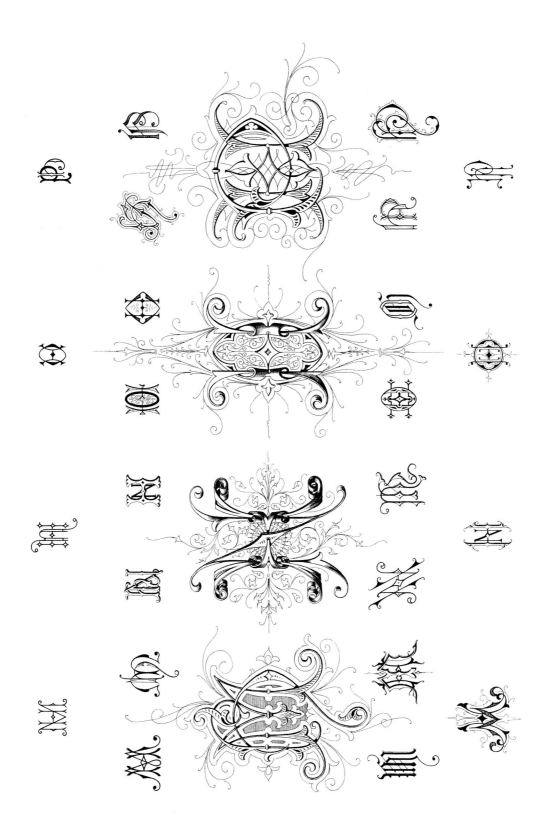

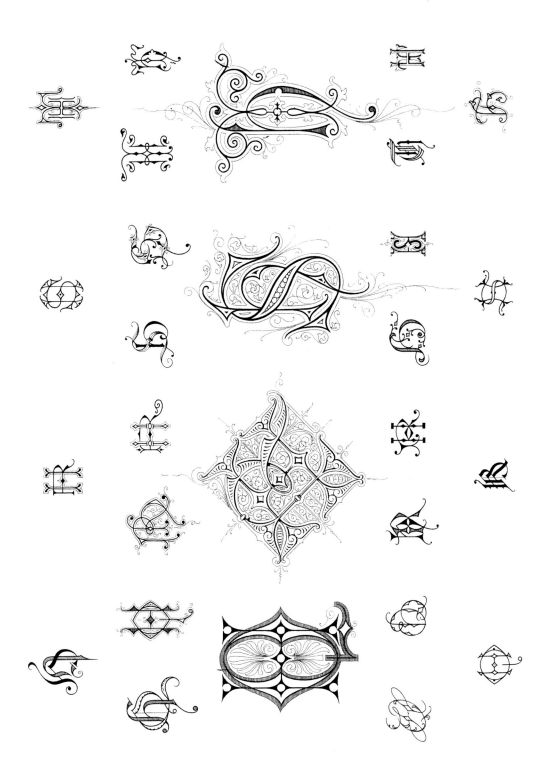

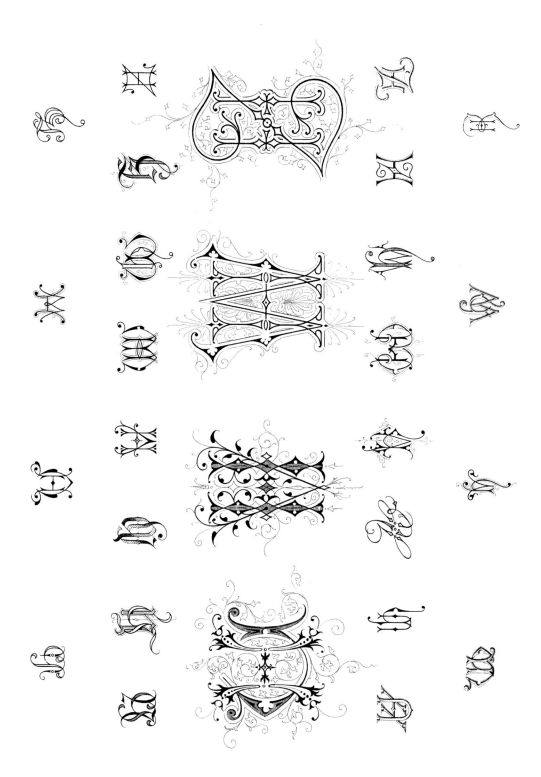

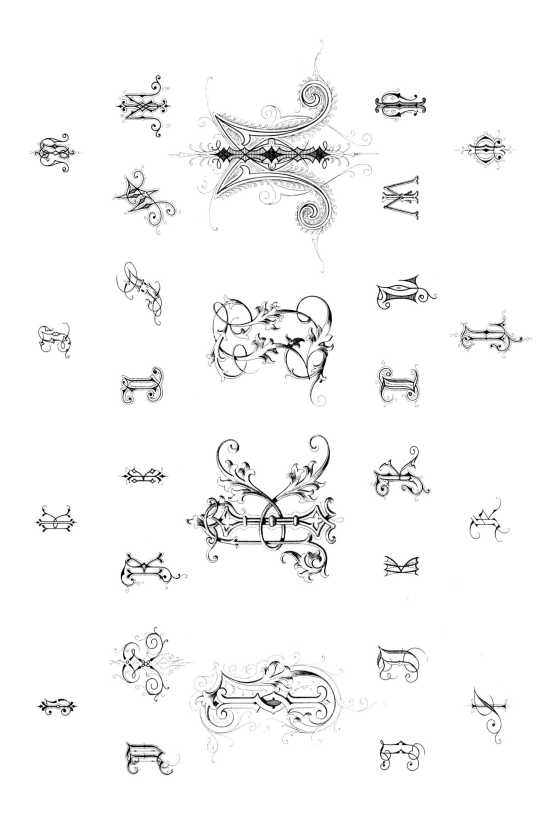

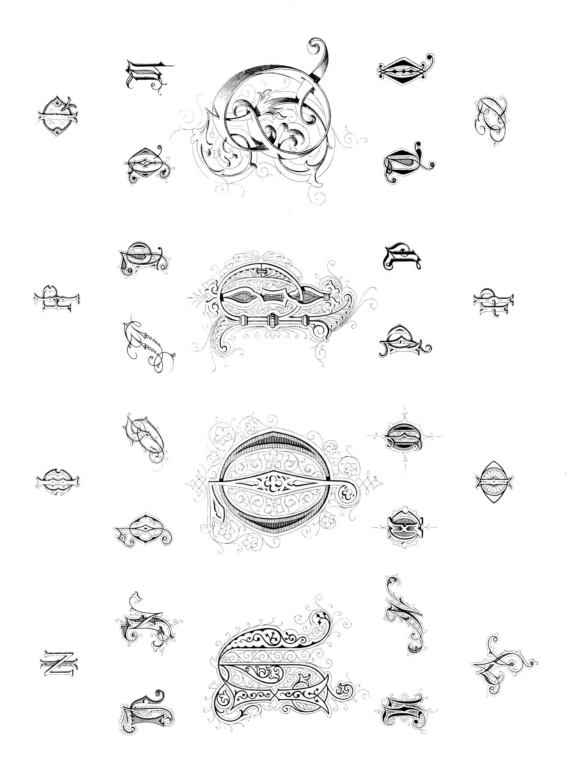

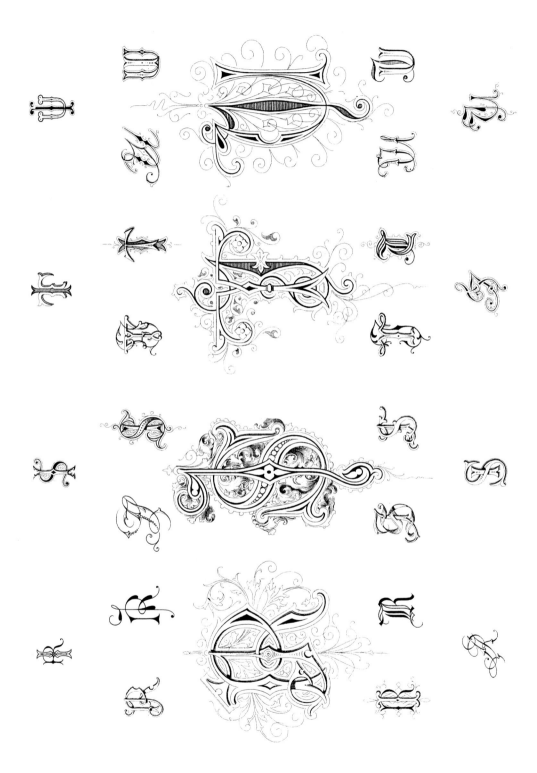

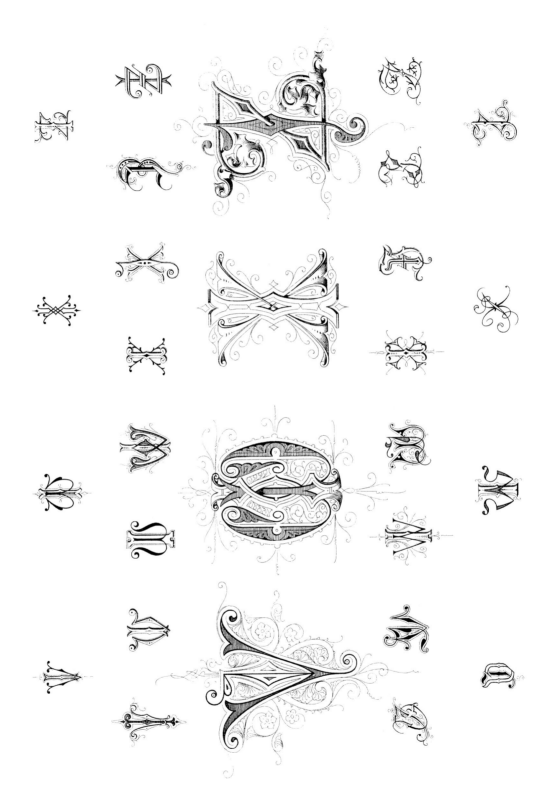

64

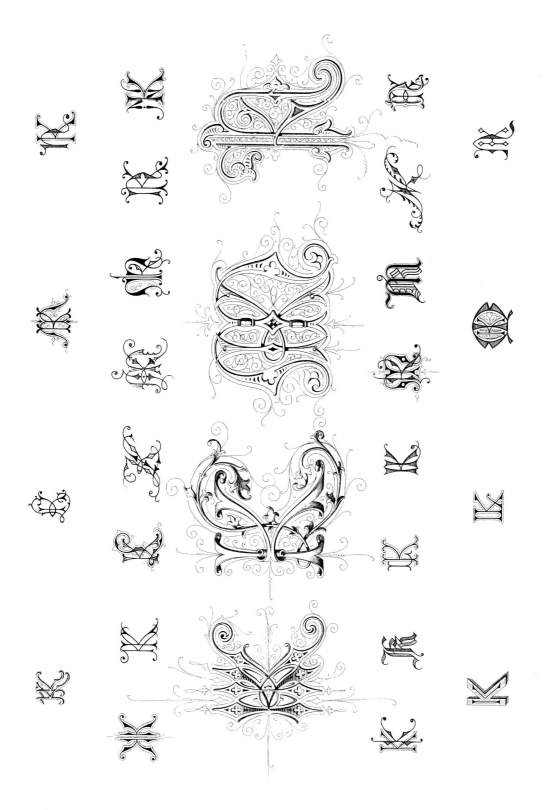

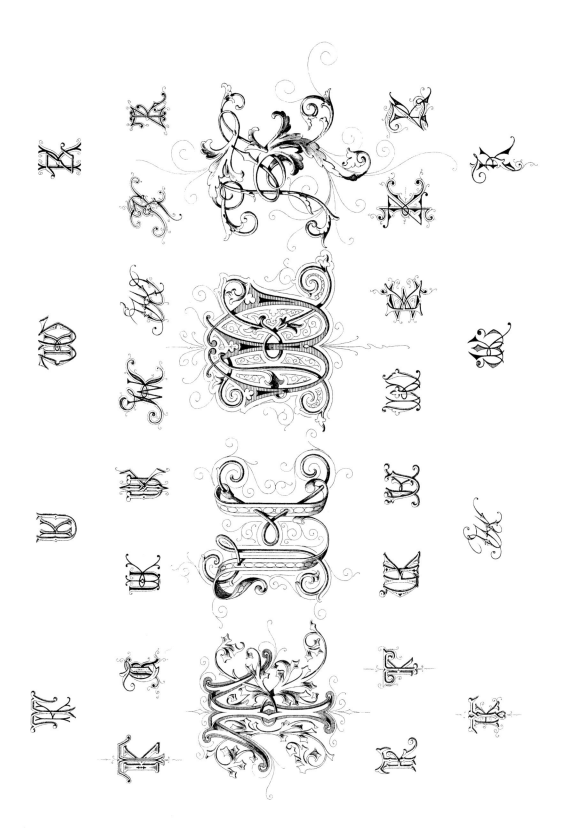

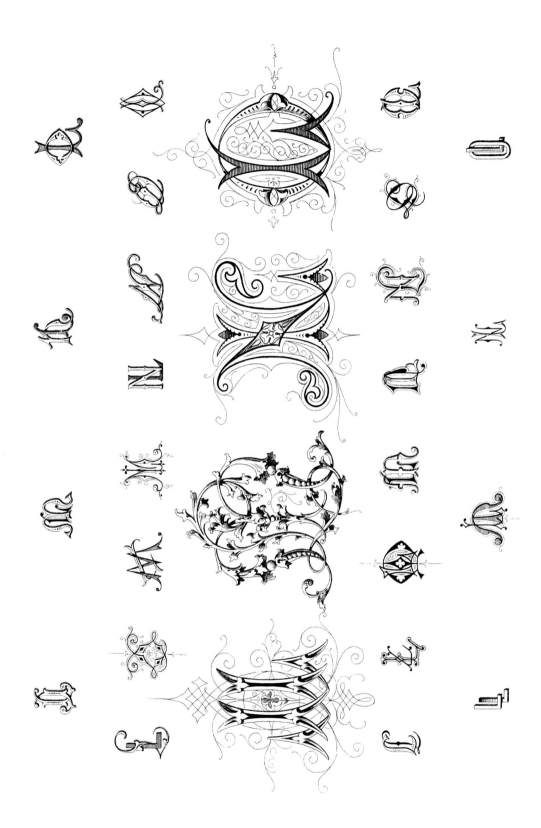

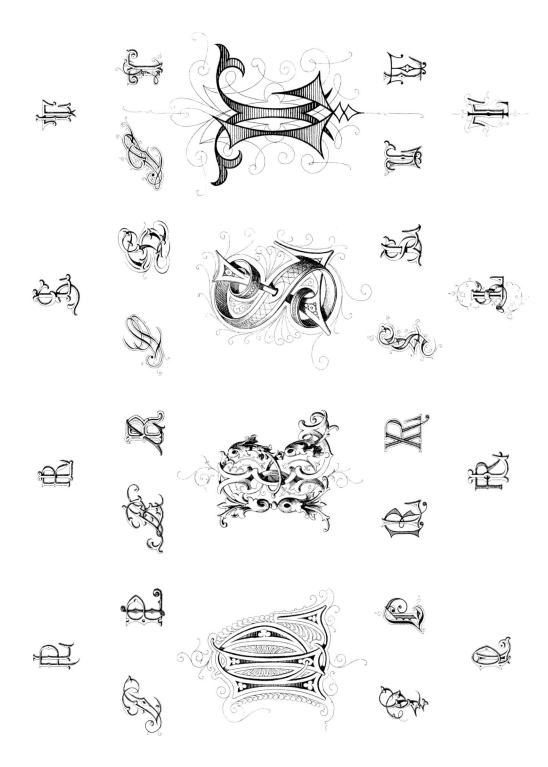

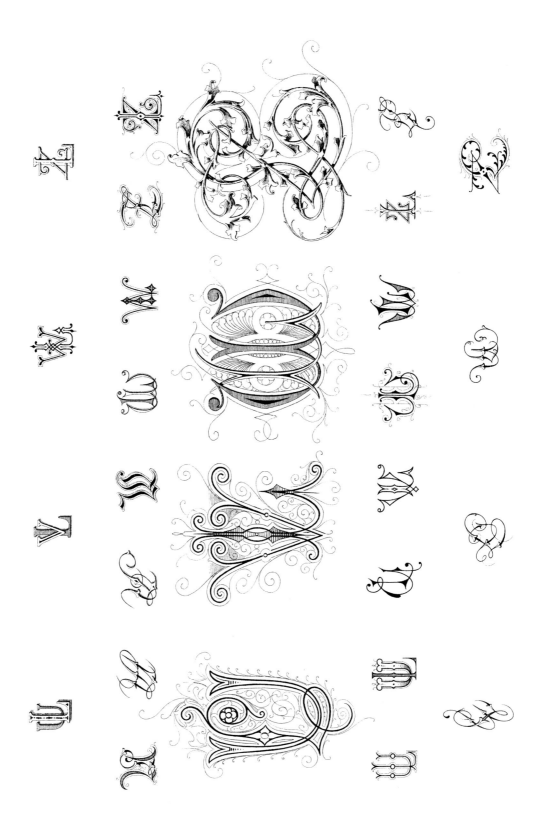

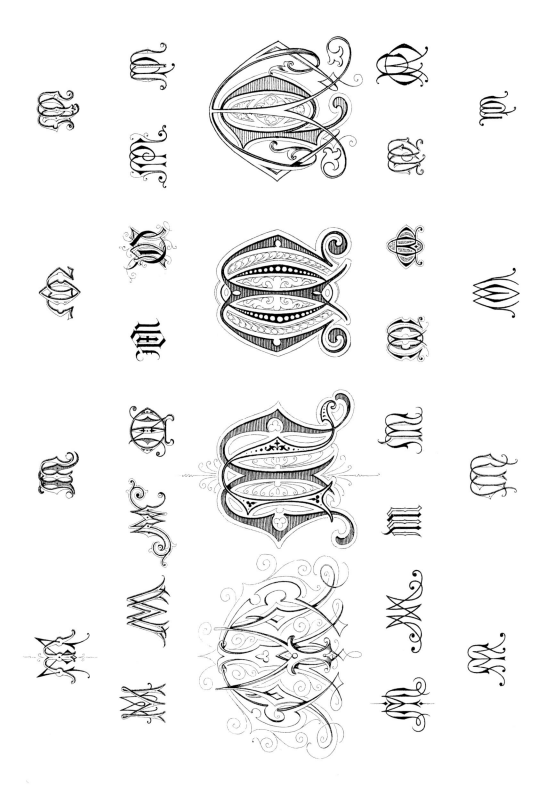

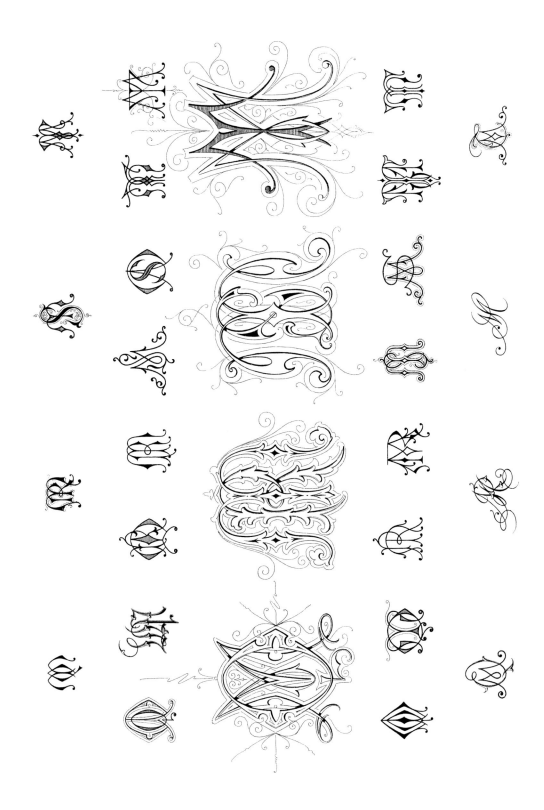

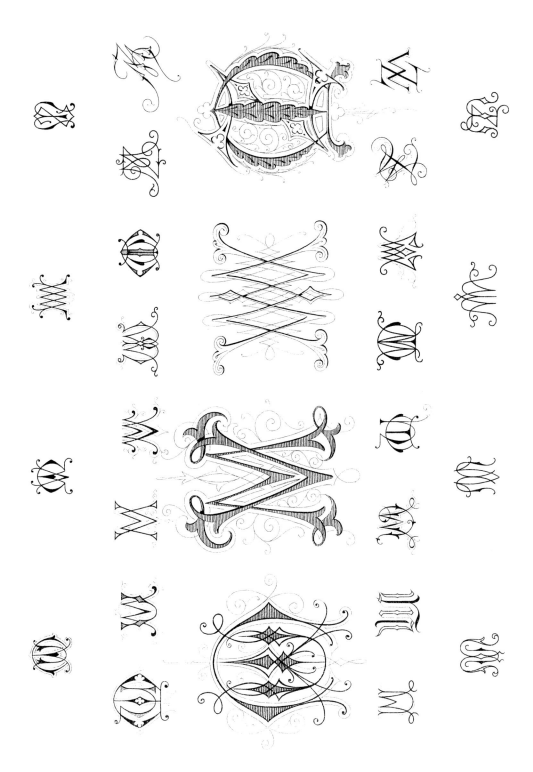

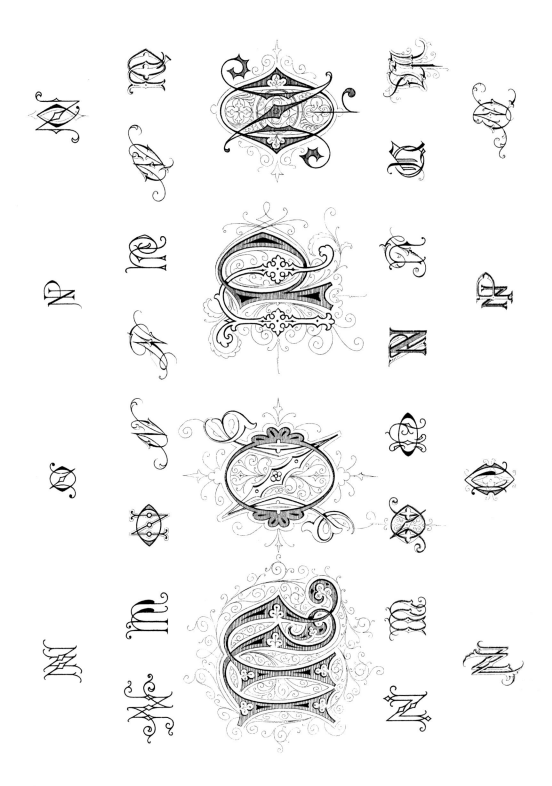

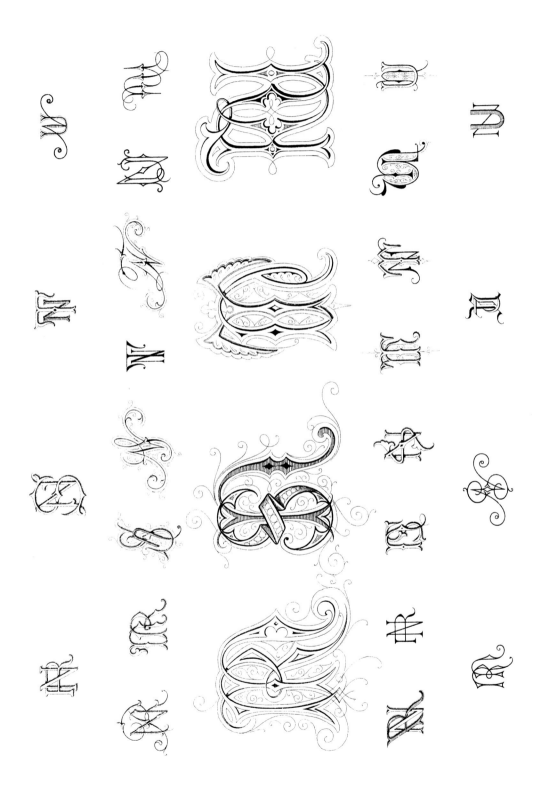

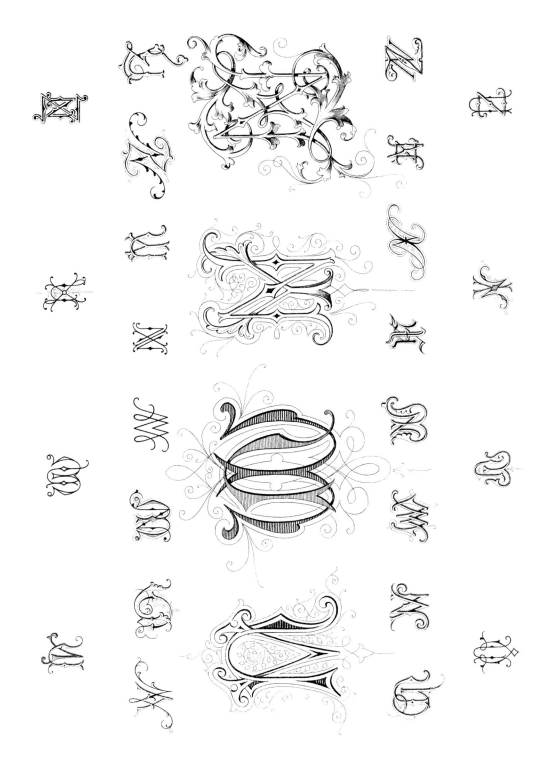

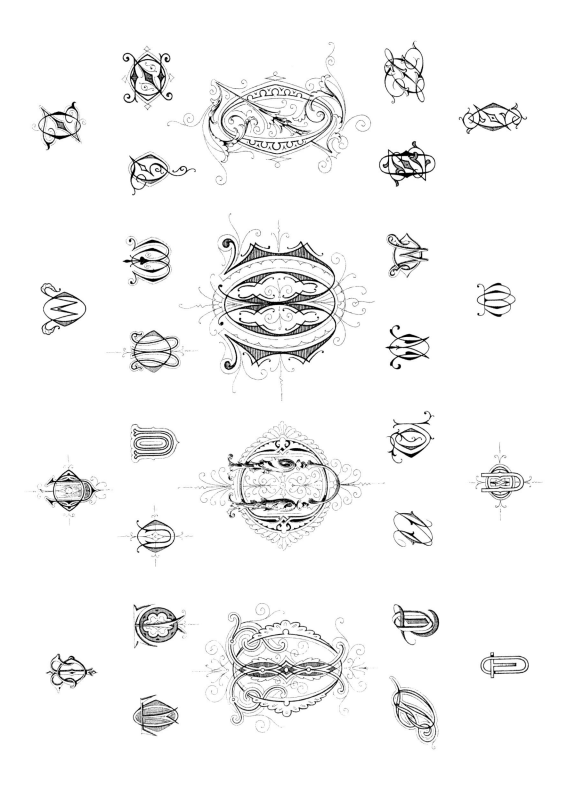

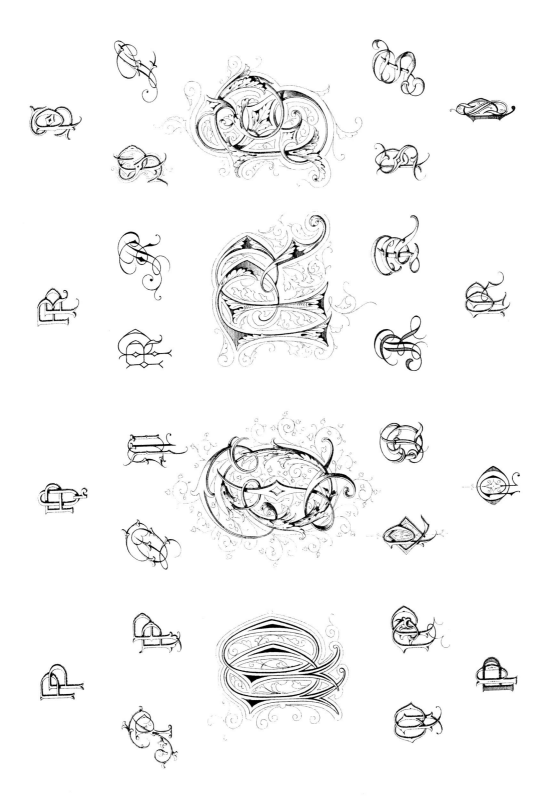

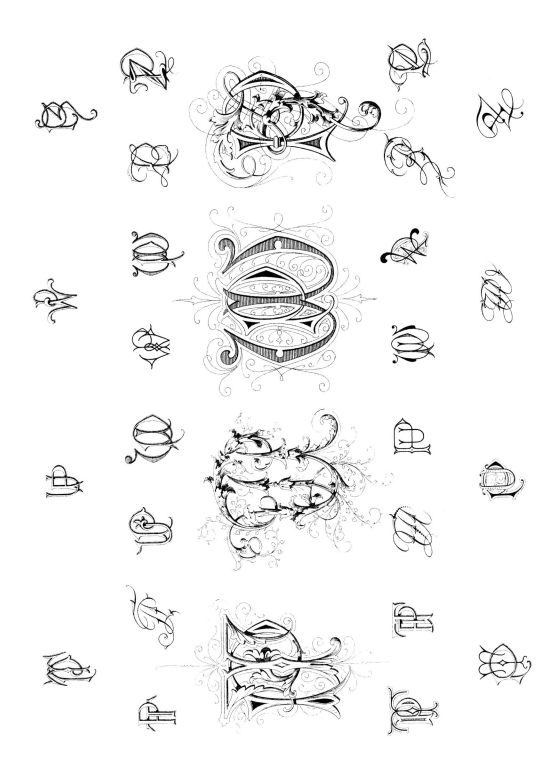

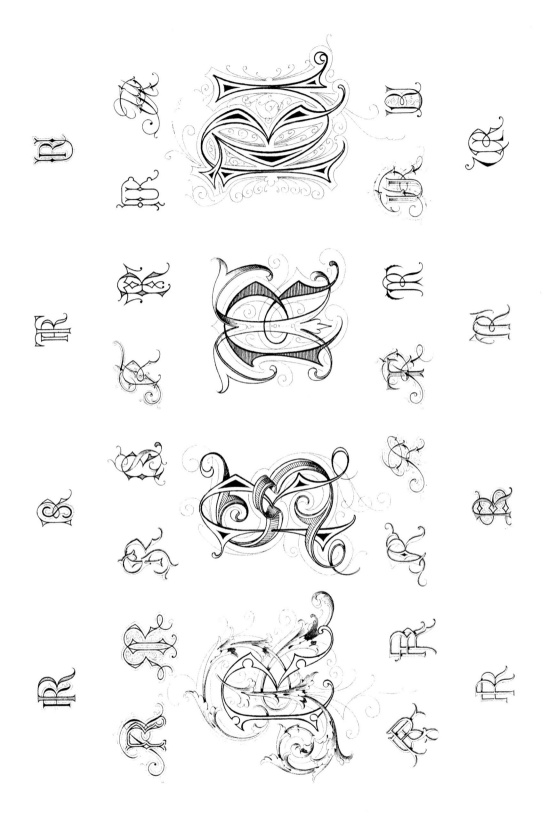

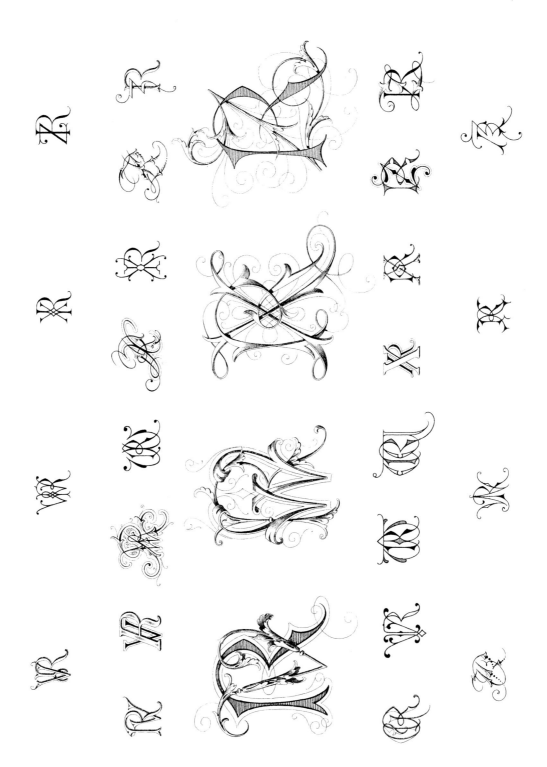

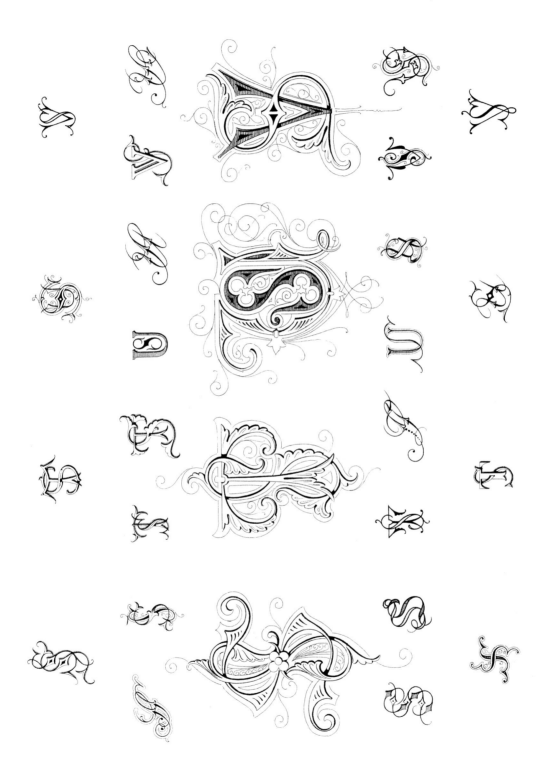

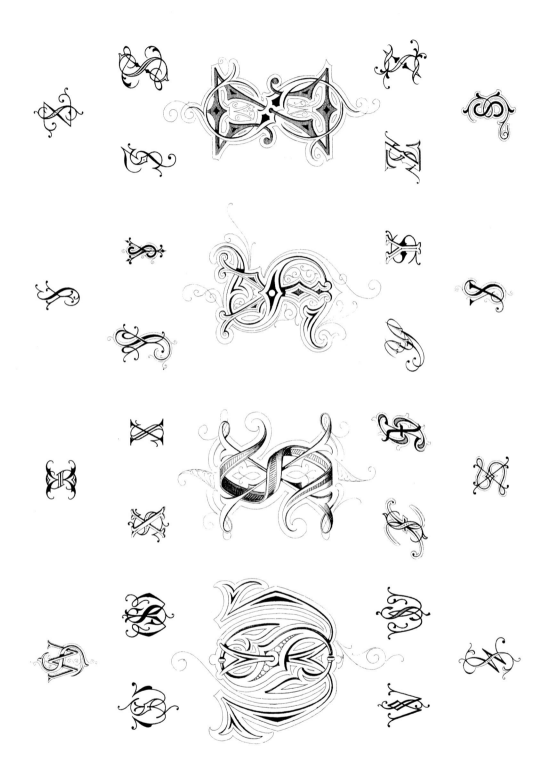

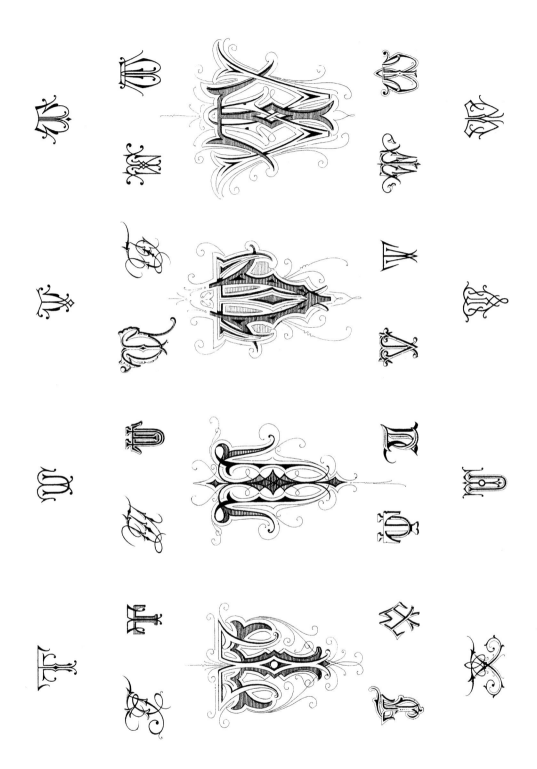

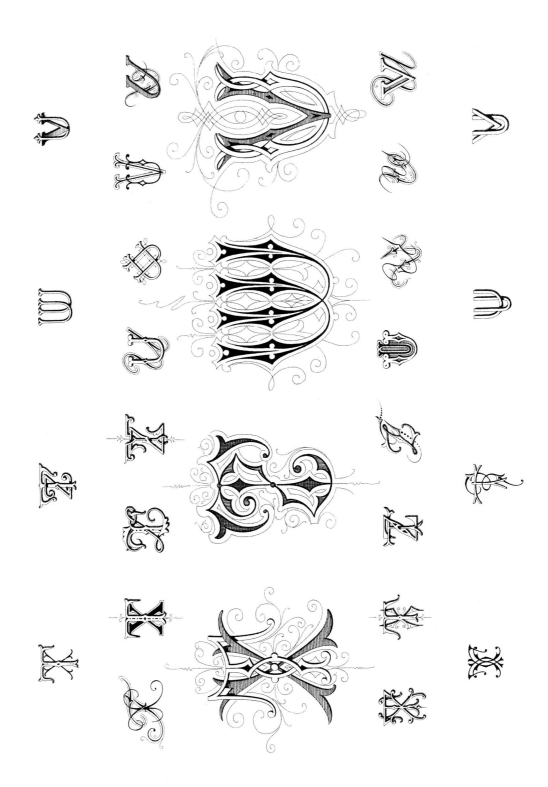

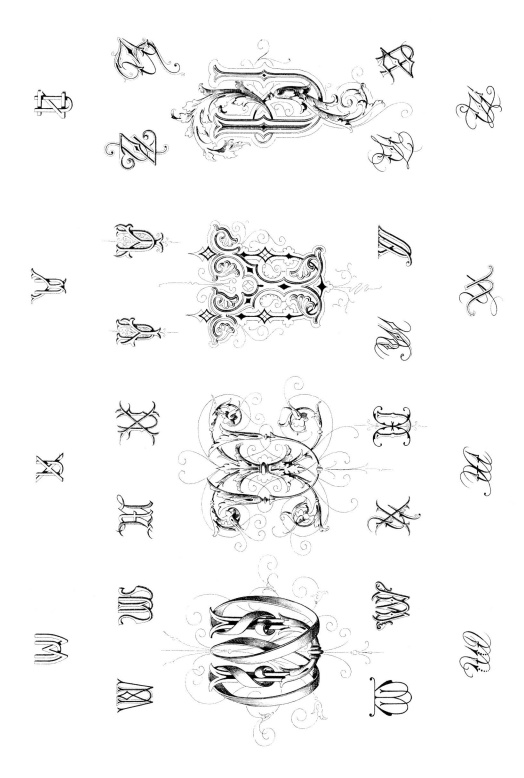

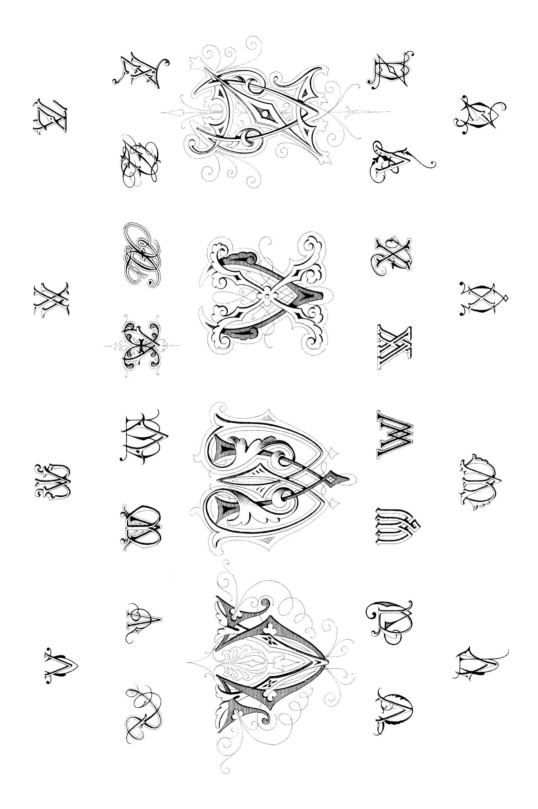

EPF       QF       FE

RS       RFP       RRF

FS       SR       CFS

AA  AA  AA

AA  AA  AA

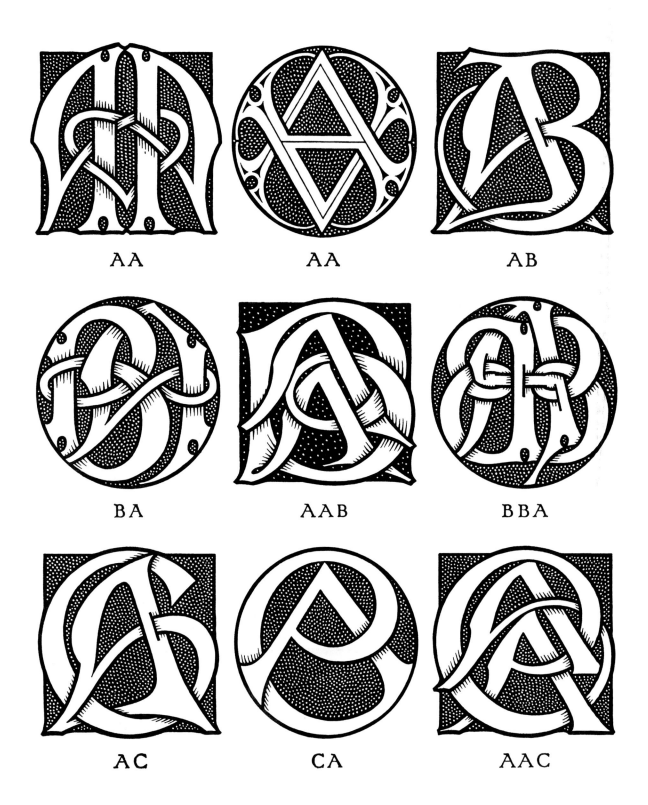

AA        AA        AB

BA        AAB        BBA

AC        CA        AAC

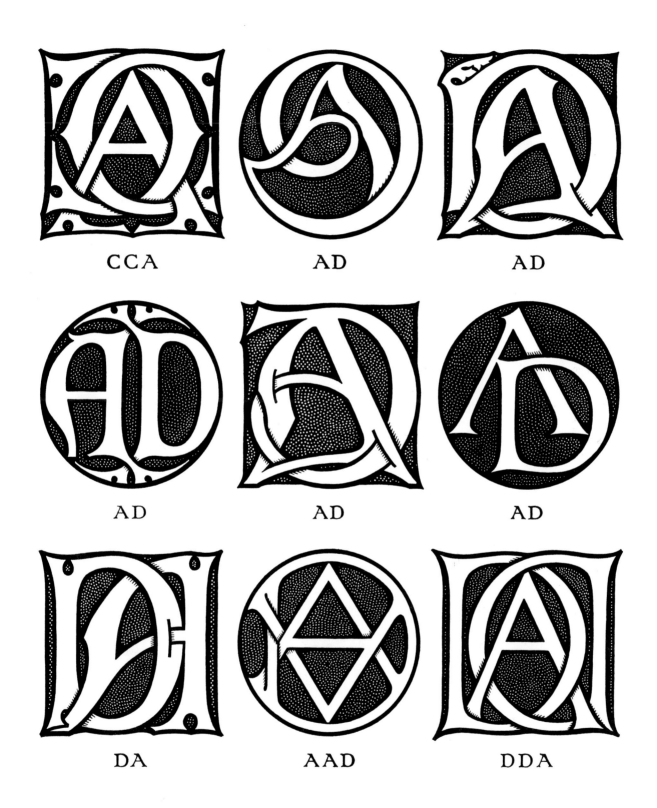

CCA  AD  AD

AD  AD  AD

DA  AAD  DDA

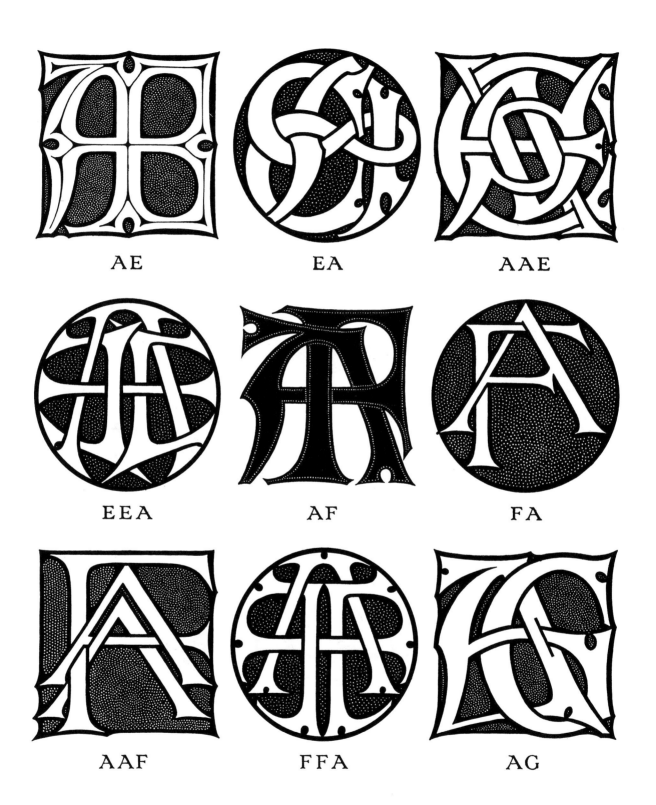

AE          EA          AAE

EEA          AF          FA

AAF          FFA          AG

GA      AAG      GGA

AH      HA      AAH

HHA      AI      AAI

IIA   AJ   JA

AAJ   JJA   AK

KA   AAK   KKA

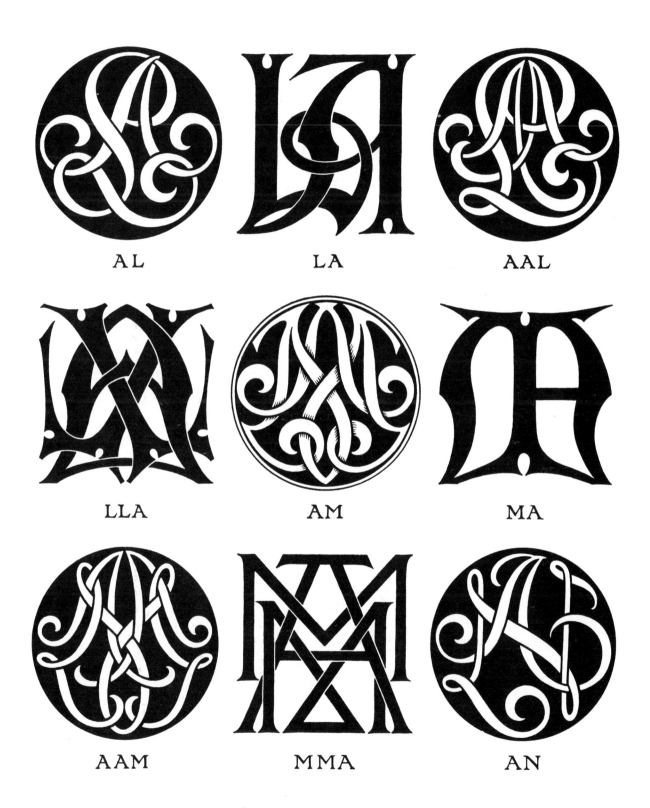

AL     LA     AAL

LLA     AM     MA

AAM     MMA     AN

NA AAN NNA

AO AAO OOA

AP PA AAP

PPA          AQ          QA

AR          RA          AAR

RRA          AS          SA

AAS  SSA  AT

TA  TTA  AU

UA  AAU  UUA

AV    VA    AW

WA    AAW    WWA

AX    AY    AZ

BB  BC  CB

BBC  CCB  BD

DB  BBD  DDB

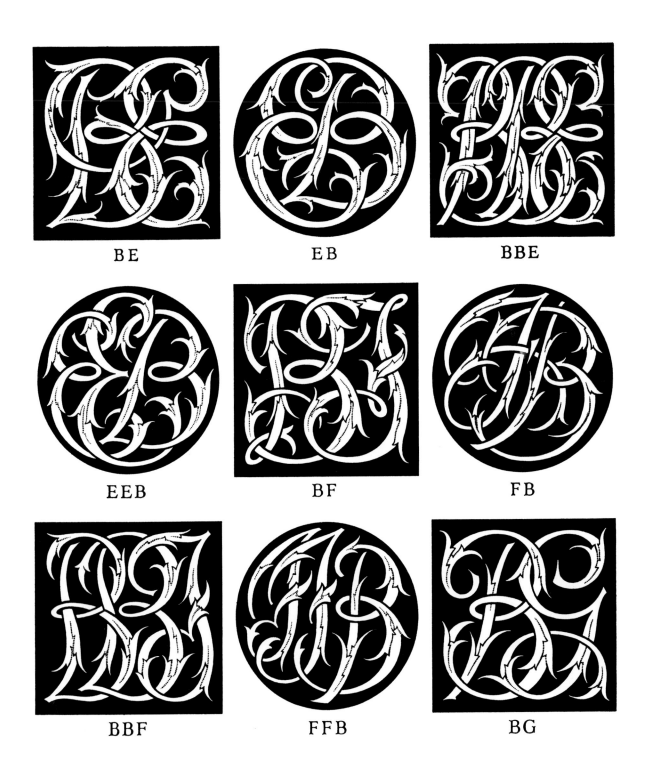

BE  EB  BBE

EEB  BF  FB

BBF  FFB  BG

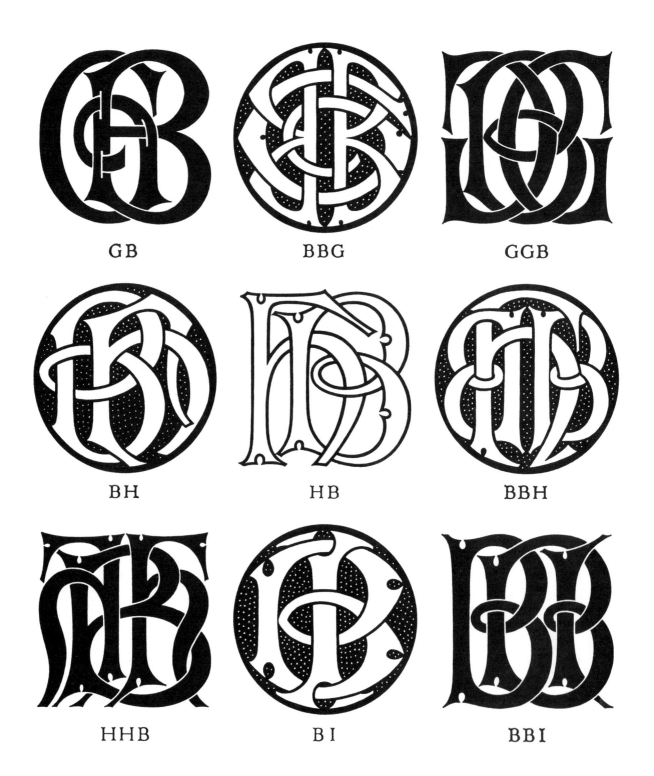

GB  BBG  GGB

BH  HB  BBH

HHB  BI  BBI

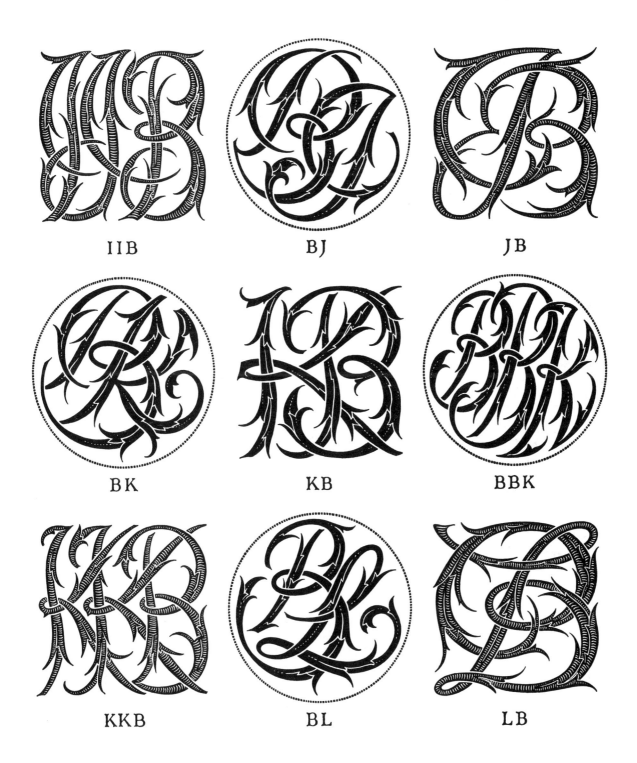

IIB      BJ      JB

BK      KB      BBK

KKB      BL      LB

BBL     LLB     BM

MB     BBM     MMB

BN     NB     BBN

NNB     BO     OB

BBO     OOB     BP

PB     BBP     PPB

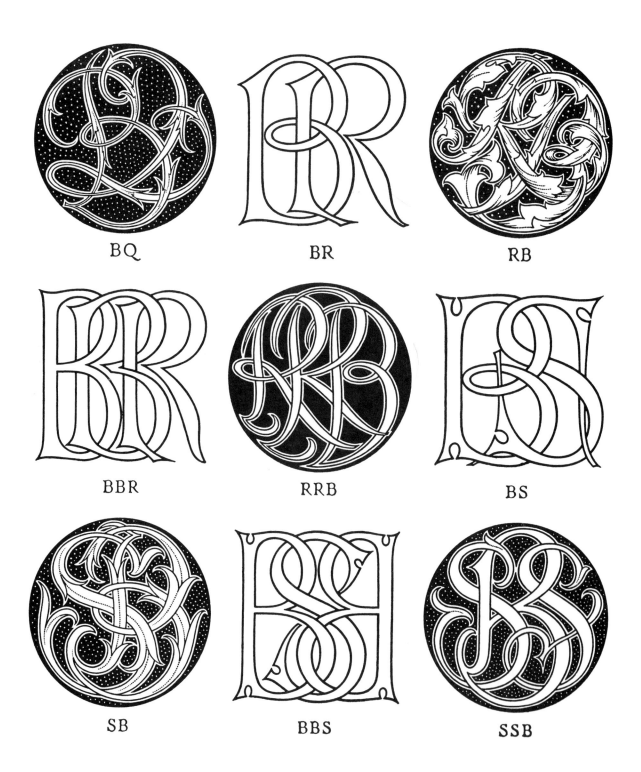

BQ

BR

RB

BBR

RRB

BS

SB

BBS

SSB

BT      TB      BBT

TTB      BU      UB

BBU      UUB      BV

VB BBV BW

WB WWB BBW

BX BY BZ

CC          DC          CD

CCD         DDC         CE

EC          CCE         EEC

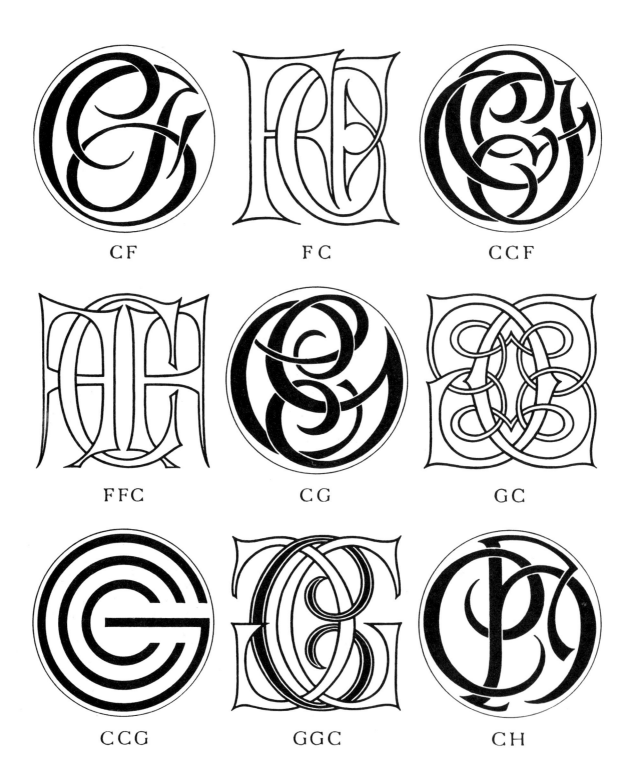

CF    F C    CCF

FFC    CG    GC

CCG    GGC    CH

HC        CCH        HHC

CI        IC        CCI

IIC        CJ        JC

CCJ · JJC · CK

KC · CCK · KKC

CL · LC · CCL

LLC      CM      MC

CCM      MMC      CN

NC      CCN      NNC

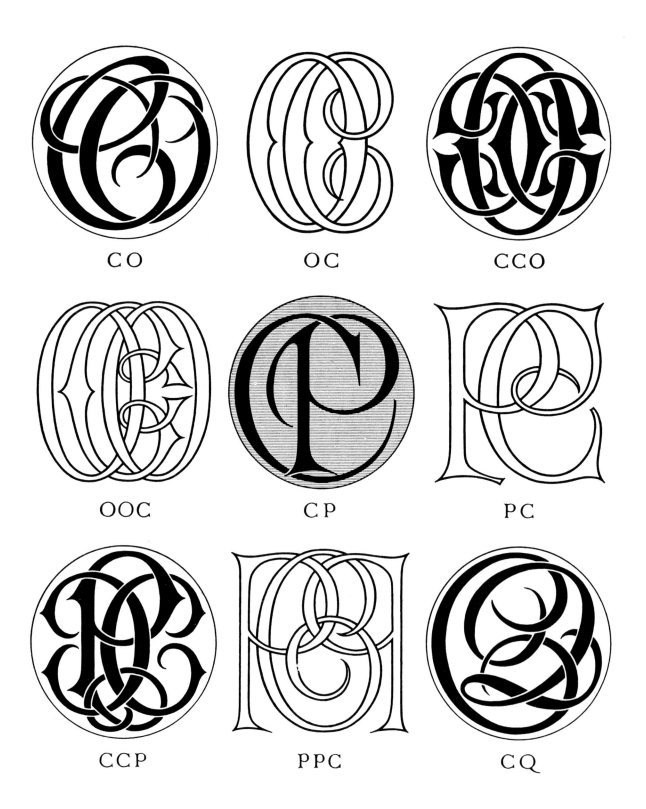

CO     OC     CCO

OOC     CP     PC

CCP     PPC     CQ

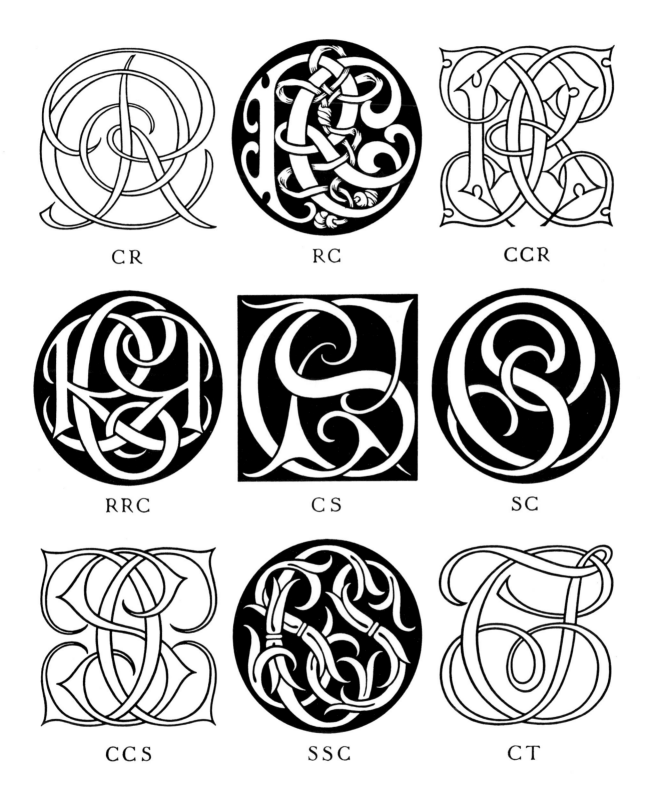

CR  RC  CCR

RRC  CS  SC

CCS  SSC  CT

TC        CCT        TTC

CU        UC        CCU

UUC        CV        VC

CCV      VVC      CW

WC      CCW      WWC

CX      CY      CZ

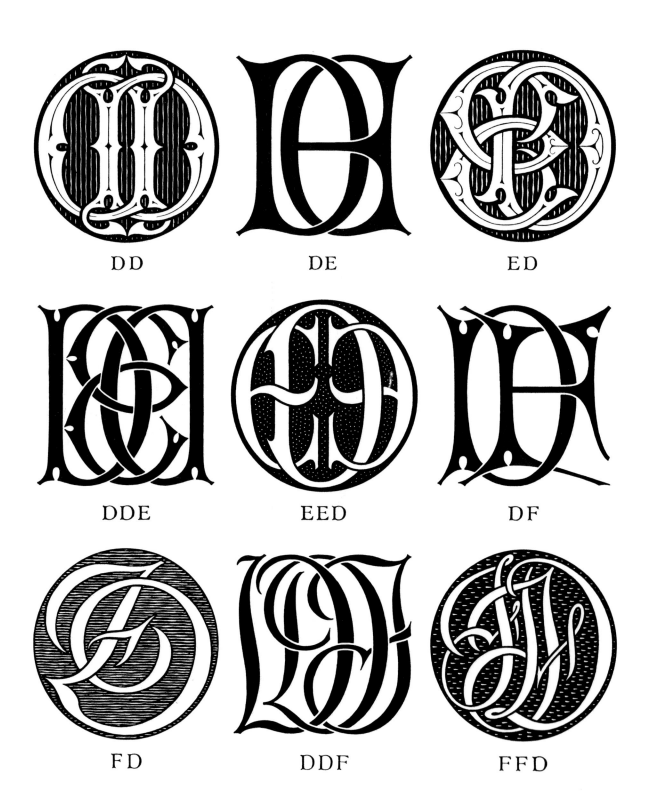

DD            DE            ED

DDE           EED           DF

FD            DDF           FFD

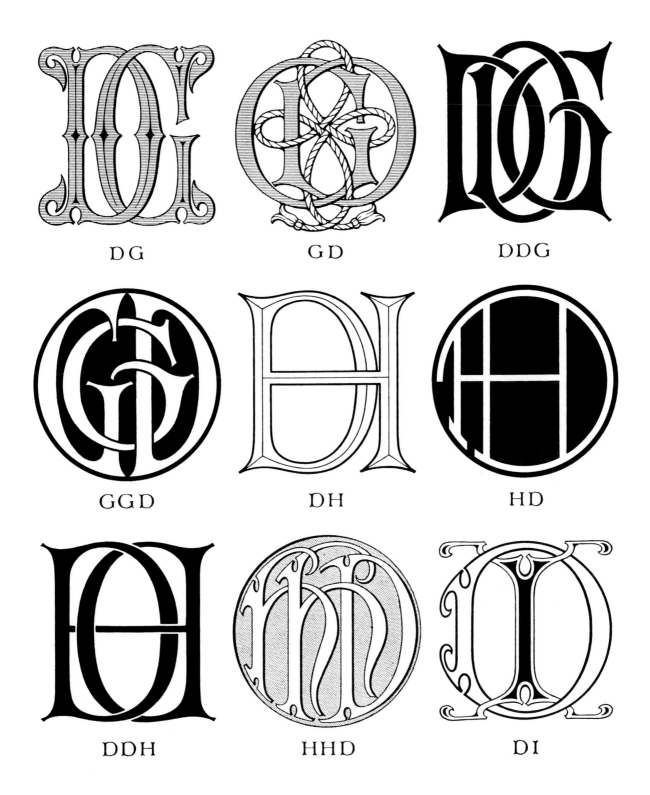

DG        GD        DDG

GGD        DH        HD

DDH        HHD        DI

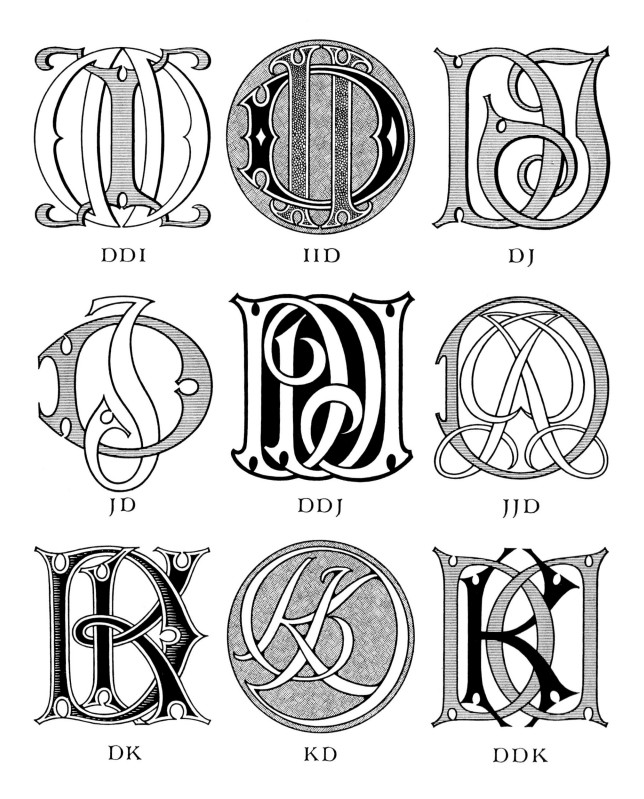

DDI IID DJ

JD DDJ JJD

DK KD DDK

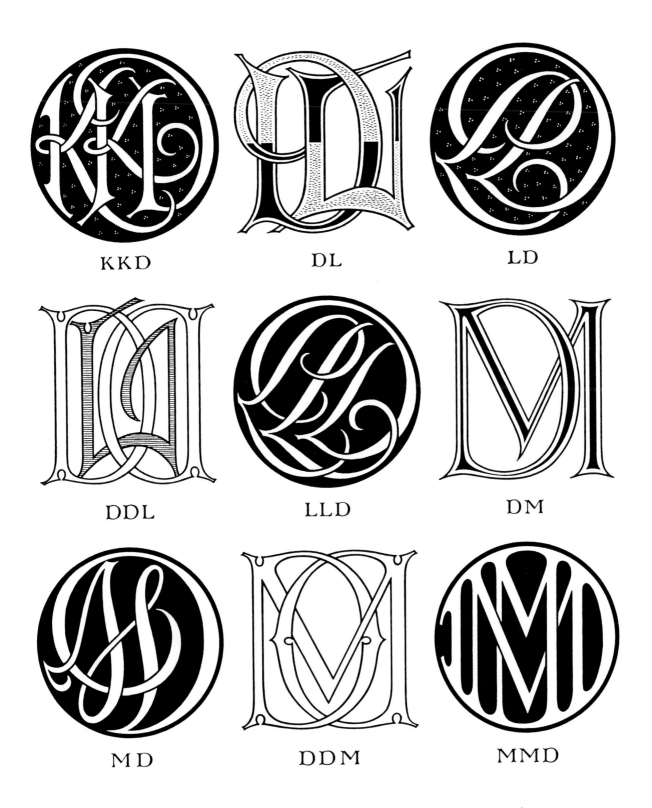

KKD        DL        LD

DDL        LLD        DM

MD        DDM        MMD

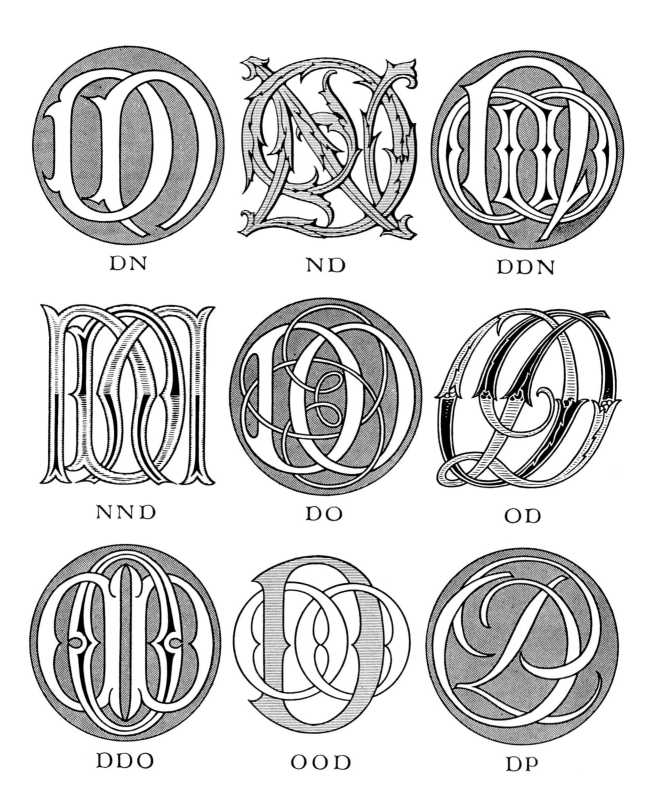

DN          ND          DDN

NND          DO          OD

DDO          OOD          DP

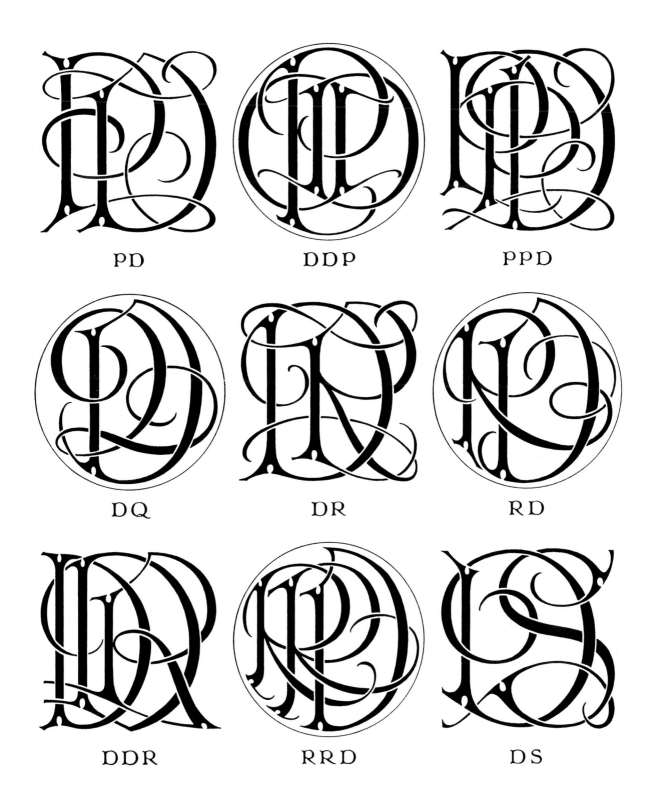

PD        DDP        PPD

DQ        DR        RD

DDR        RRD        DS

SD    DDS    SSD

DT    TD    DDT

TTD    DU    UD

DDU UUD DV

VD DW WD

DDW WWD DX

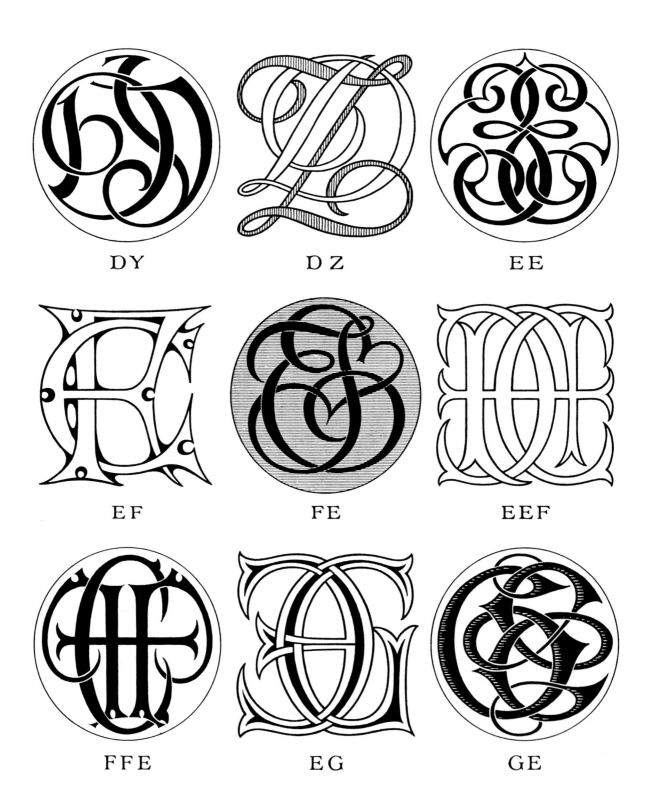

DY  DZ  EE

EF  FE  EEF

FFE  EG  GE

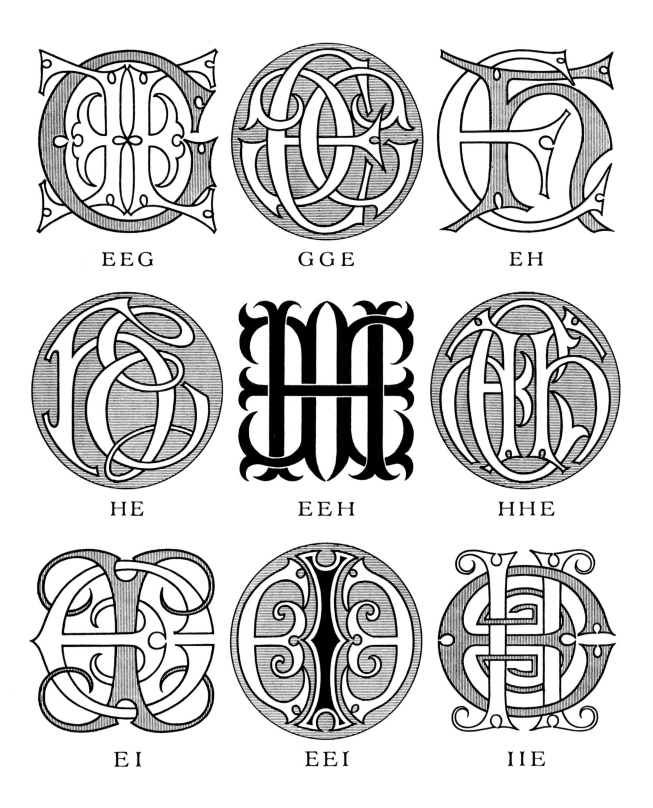

EEG         GGE         EH

HE         EEH         HHE

EI         EEI         IIE

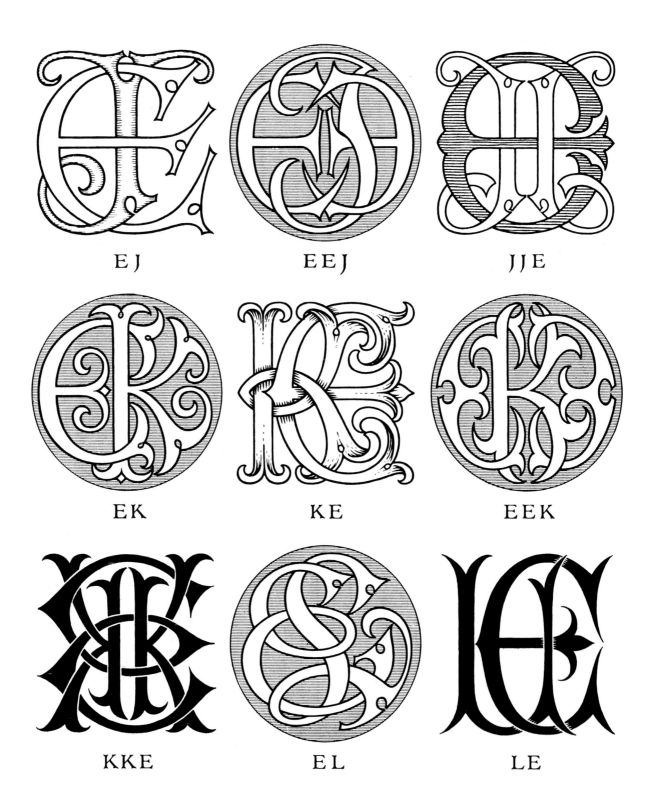

EJ          EEJ         JJE

EK          KE          EEK

KKE         EL          LE

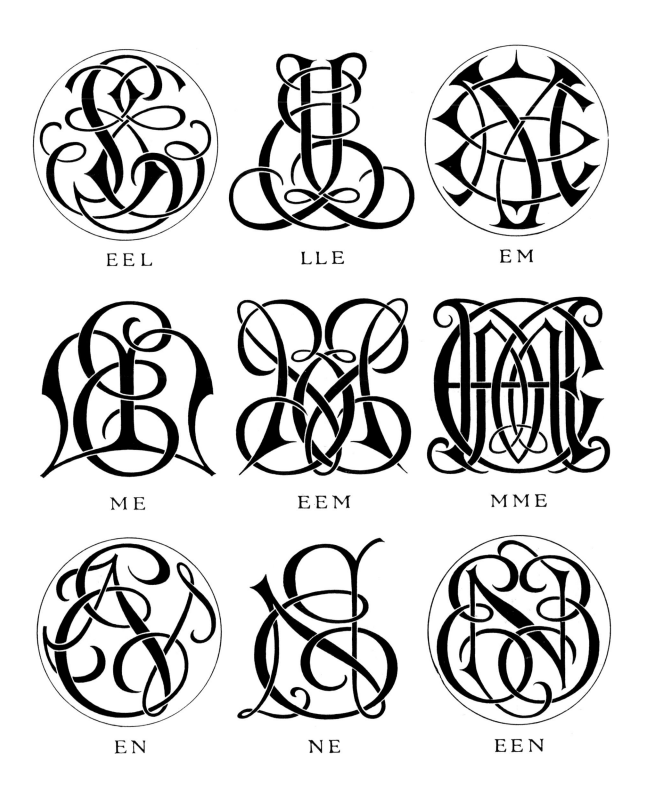

EEL  LLE  EM

ME  EEM  MME

EN  NE  EEN

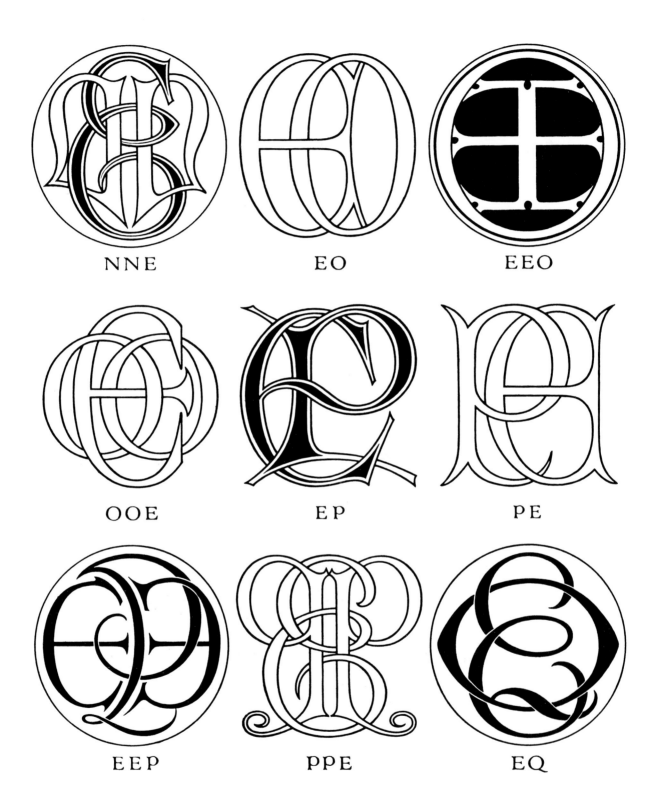

NNE     EO     EEO

OOE     EP     PE

EEP     PPE     EQ

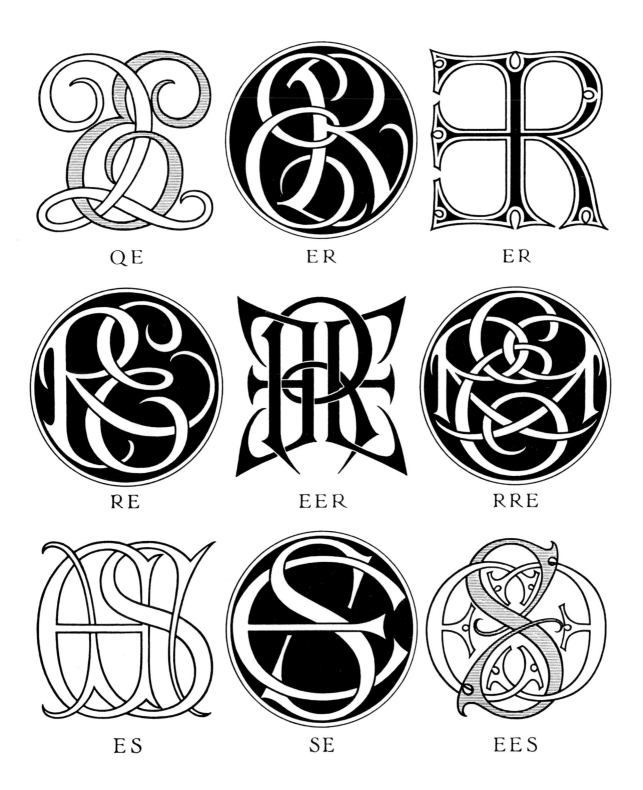

QE      ER      ER

RE      EER      RRE

ES      SE      EES

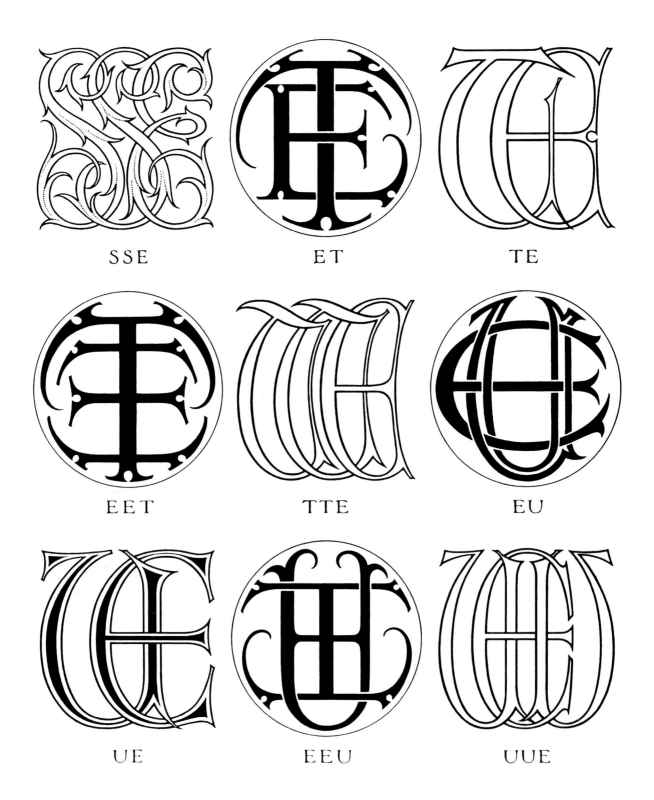

SSE      ET      TE

EET      TTE      EU

UE      EEU      UUE

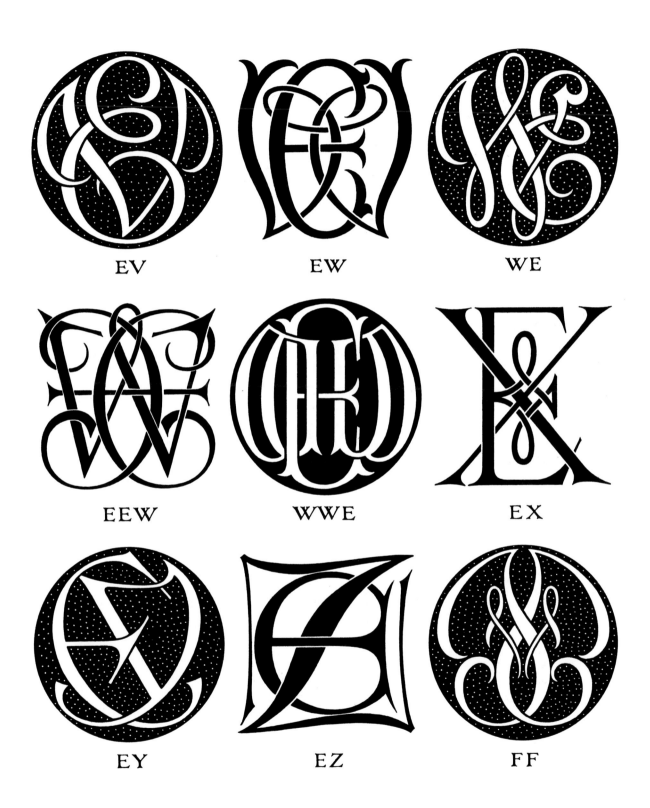

EV  EW  WE

EEW  WWE  EX

EY  EZ  FF

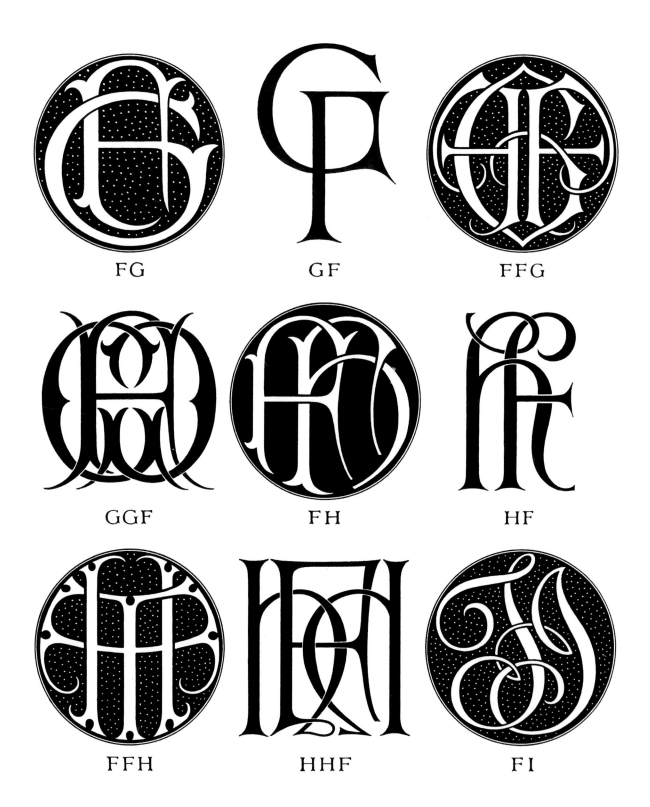

FG  GF  FFG

GGF  FH  HF

FFH  HHF  FI

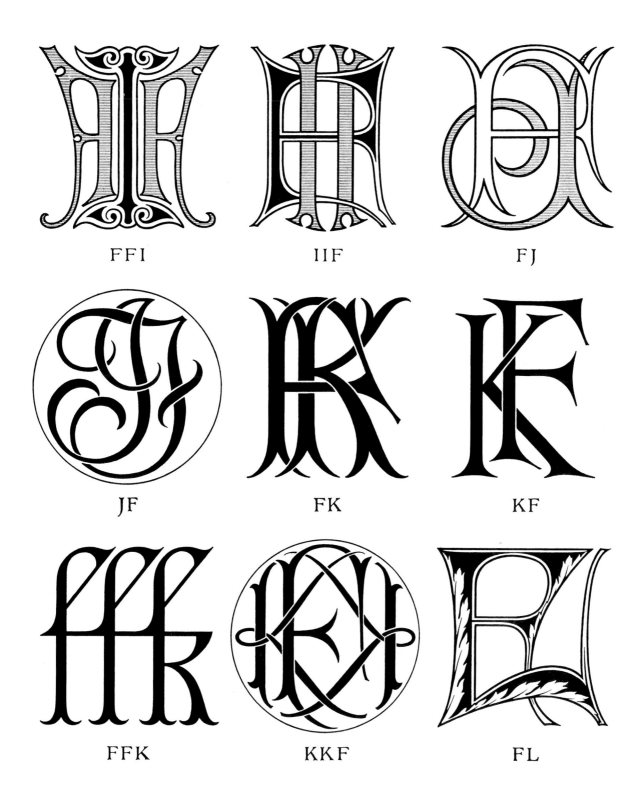

FFI      IIF      FJ

JF      FK      KF

FFK      KKF      FL

LF           FFL           LLF

FM           MF           FFM

MMF           FN           NF

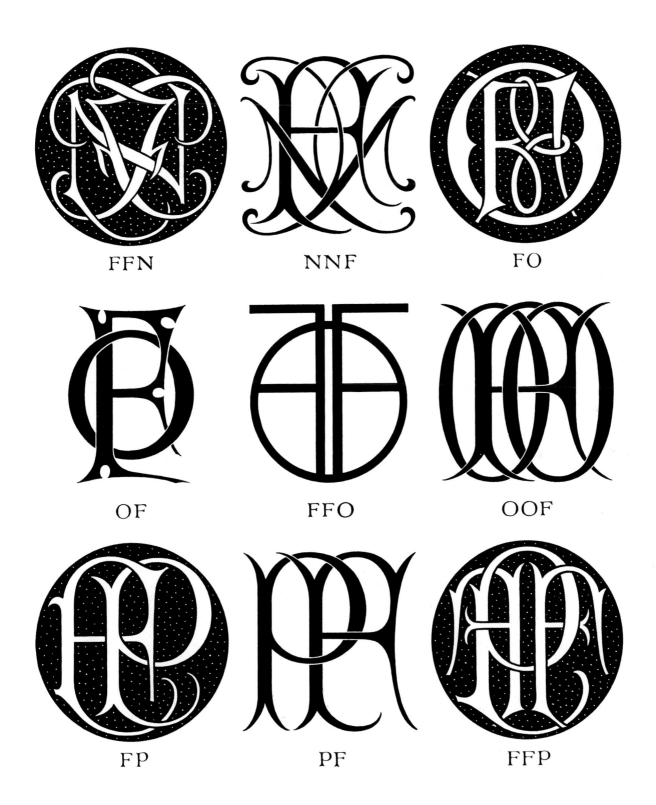

FFN     NNF     FO

OF     FFO     OOF

FP     PF     FFP

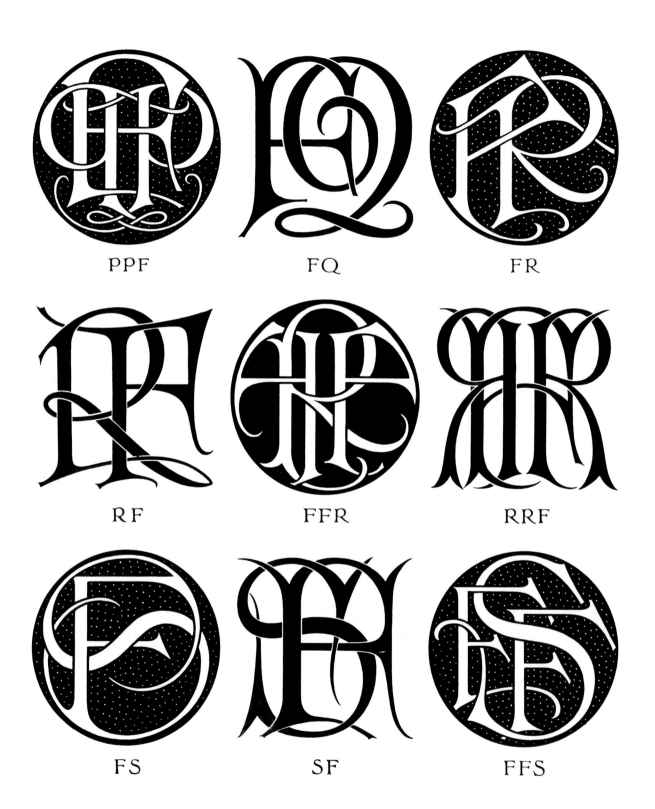

PPF   FQ   FR

RF   FFR   RRF

FS   SF   FFS

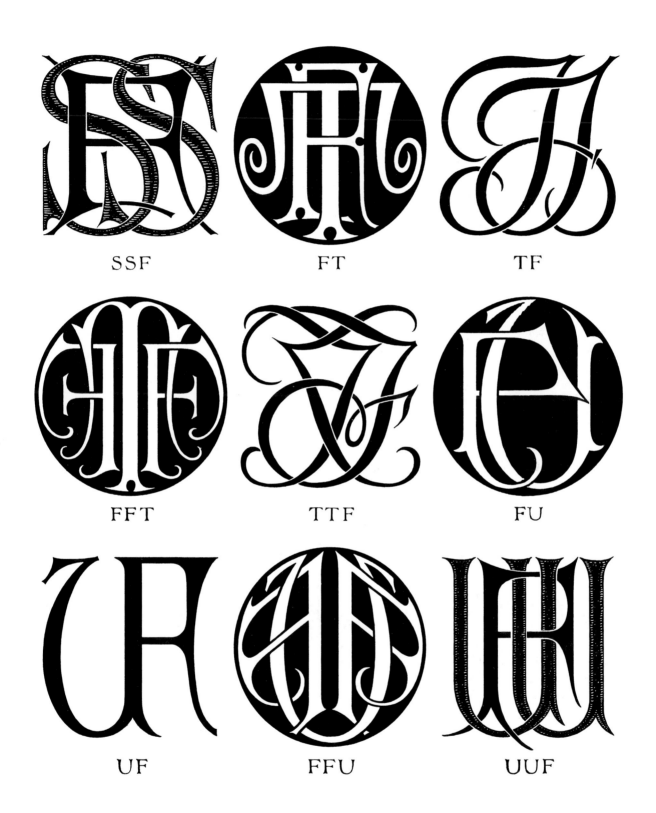

SSF      FT      TF

FFT      TTF      FU

UF      FFU      UUF

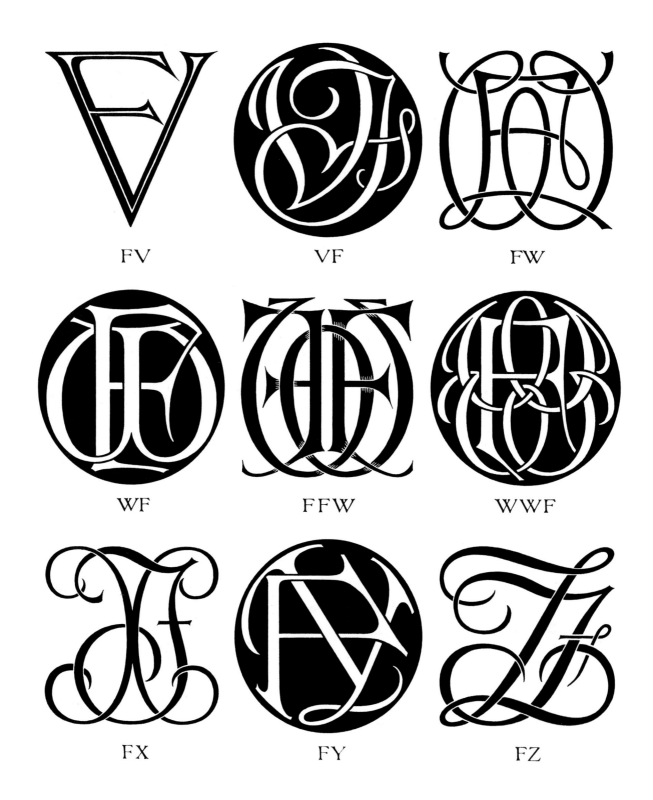

FV   VF   FW

WF   FFW   WWF

FX   FY   FZ

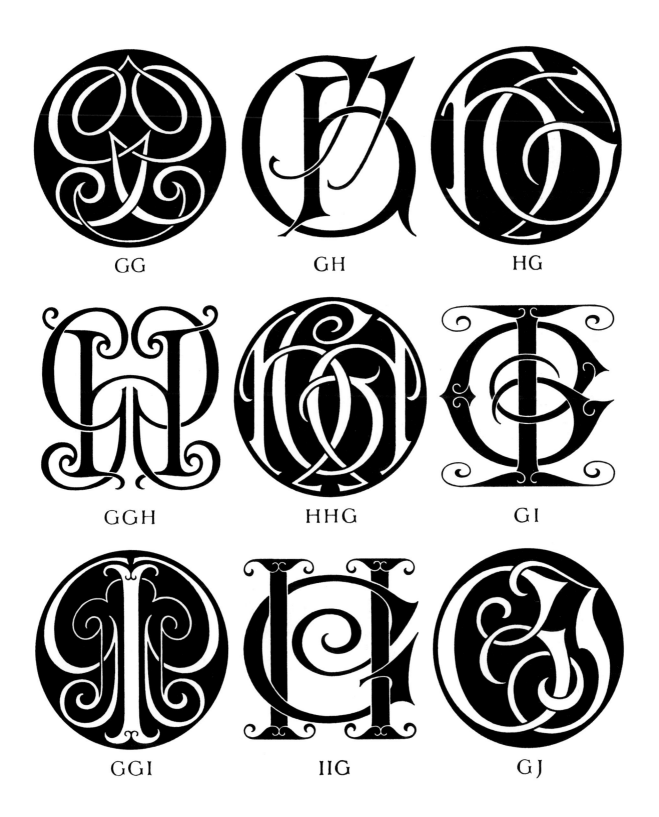

GG       GH       HG

GGH       HHG       GI

GGI       IIG       GJ

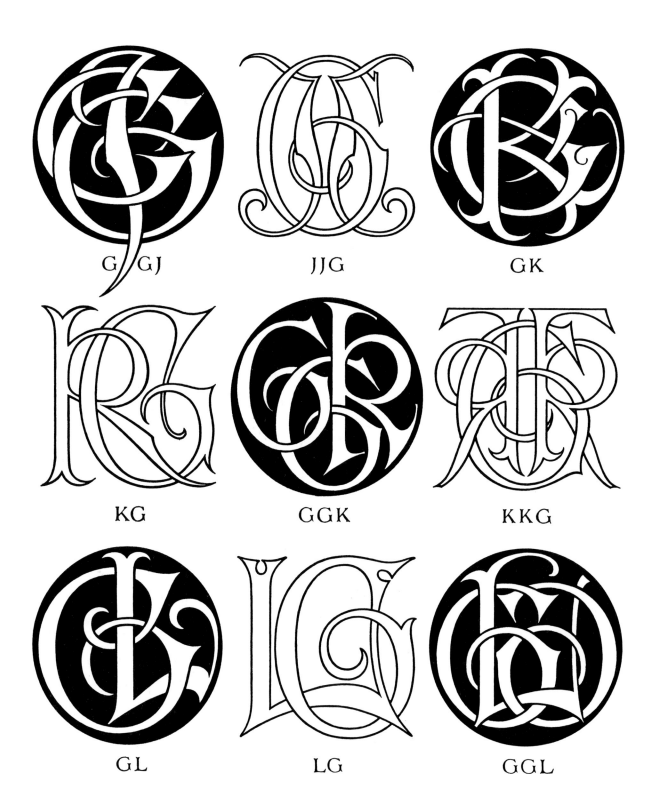

G GJ  JJG  GK

KG  GGK  KKG

GL  LG  GGL

LLG        GM        MG

GGM        MMG        GN

NG        GGN        NNG

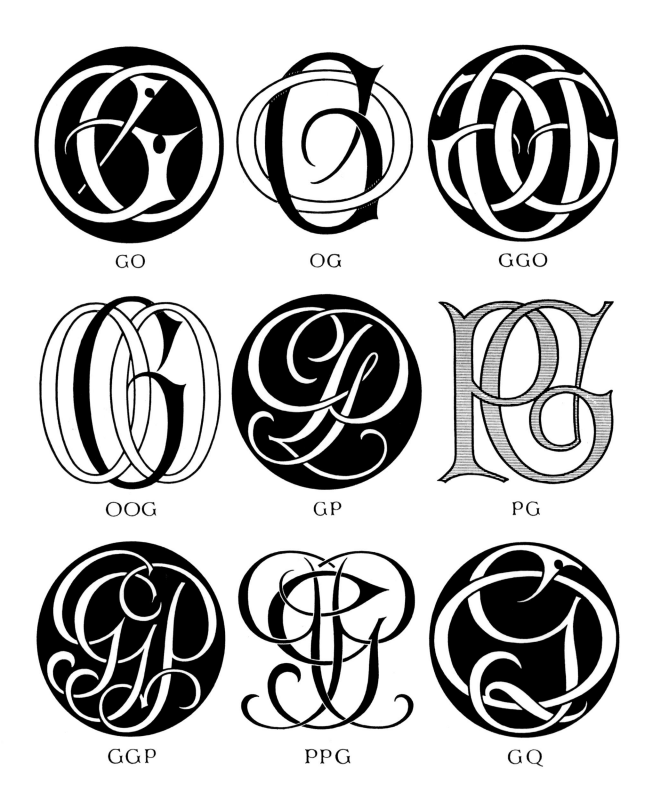

GO      OG      GGO

OOG      GP      PG

GGP      PPG      GQ

QG        GR        RG

GGR        RRG        GS

SG        GGS        SSG

GT     TG     GGT

TTG     GU     UG

GGU     UUG     GV

VG GW WG

GGW WWG GX

GY GZ HH

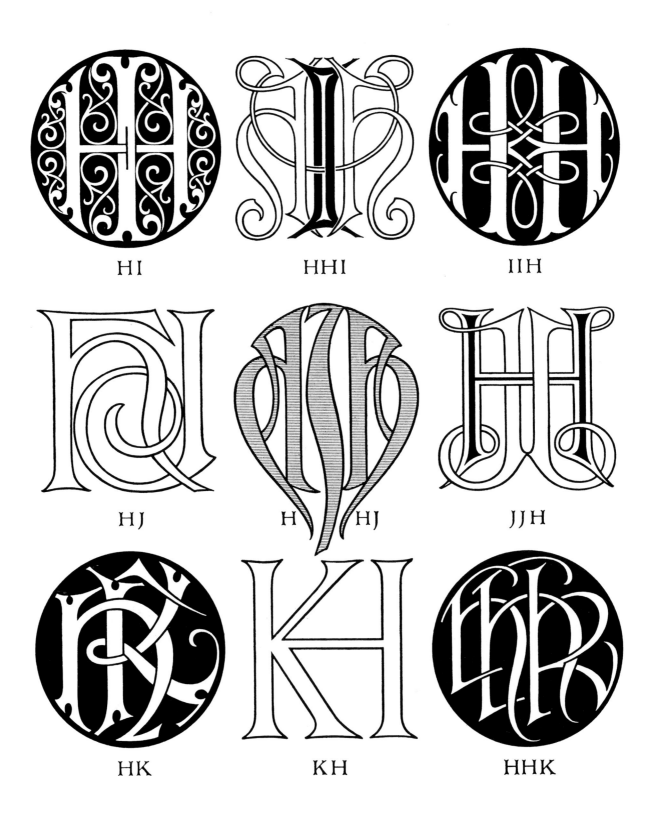

HI        HHI        IIH

HJ        H HJ        JJH

HK        KH        HHK

KKH    HL    LH

HHL    LLH    HM

MH    HHM    MMH

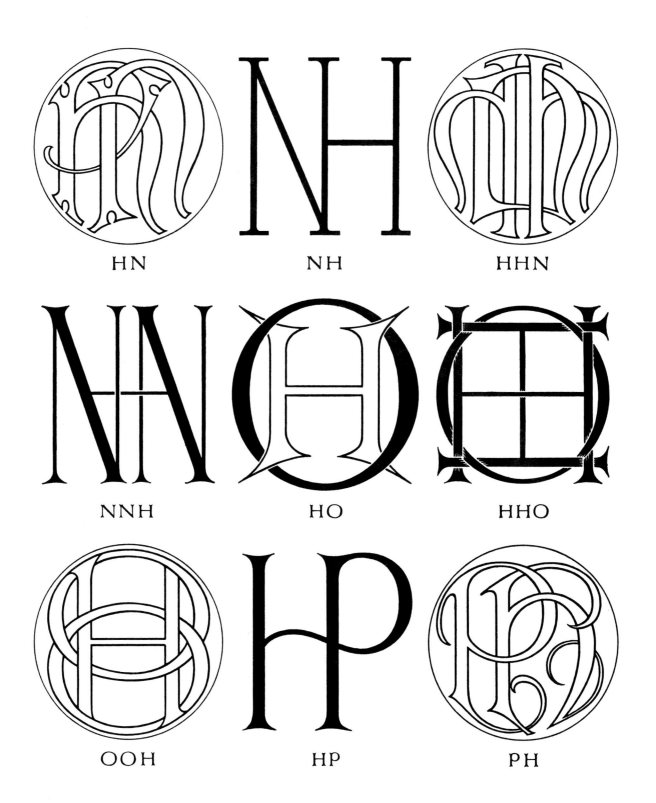

HN     NH     HHN

NNH     HO     HHO

OOH     HP     PH

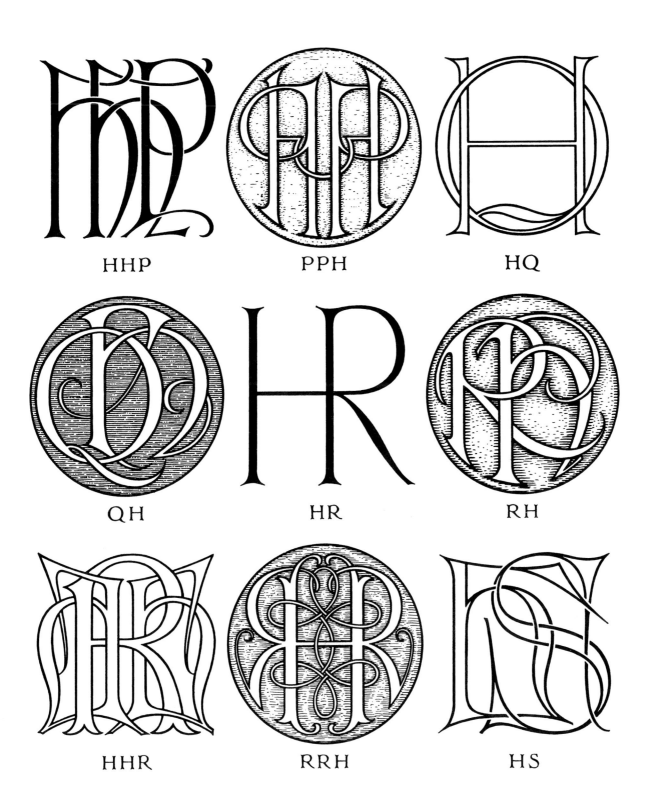

HHP PPH HQ

QH HR RH

HHR RRH HS

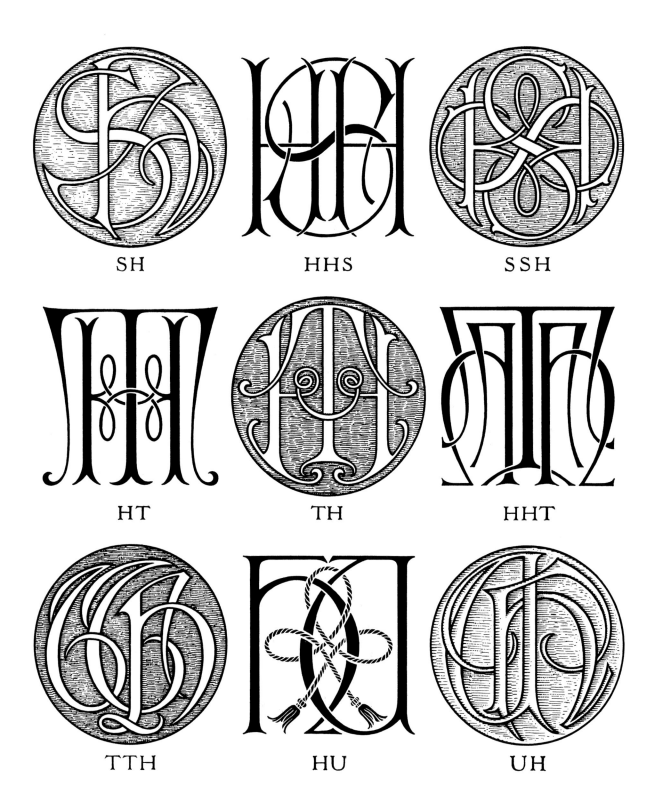

SH      HHS      SSH

HT      TH      HHT

TTH      HU      UH

HHU     UUH     HV

HW     WH     HHW

WWH     HX     HY

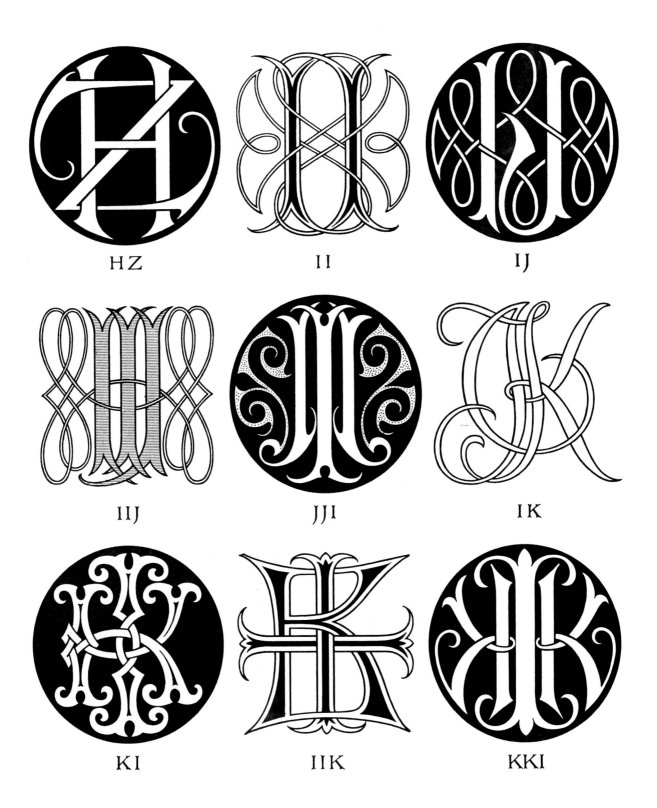

HZ

II

IJ

IIJ

JJI

IK

KI

IIK

KKI

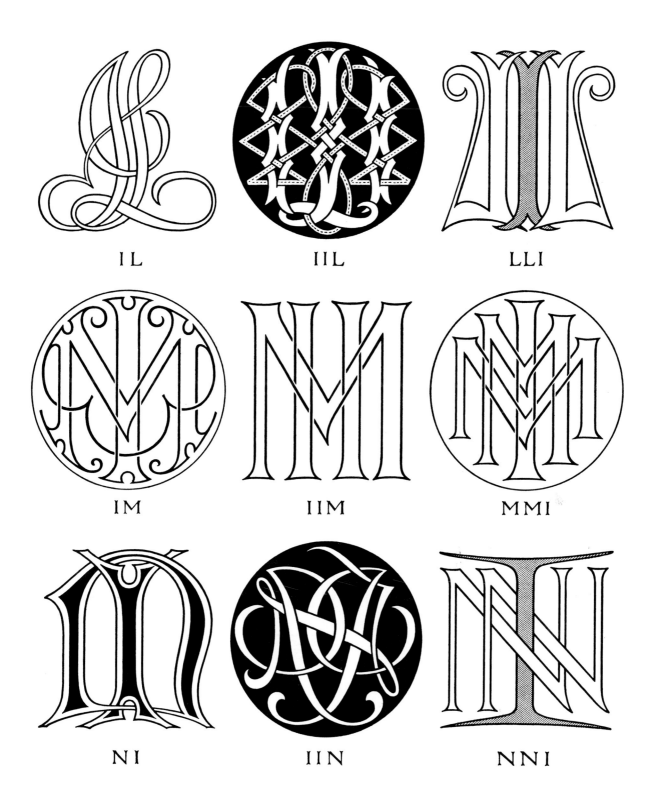

IL IIL LLI

IM IIM MMI

NI IIN NNI

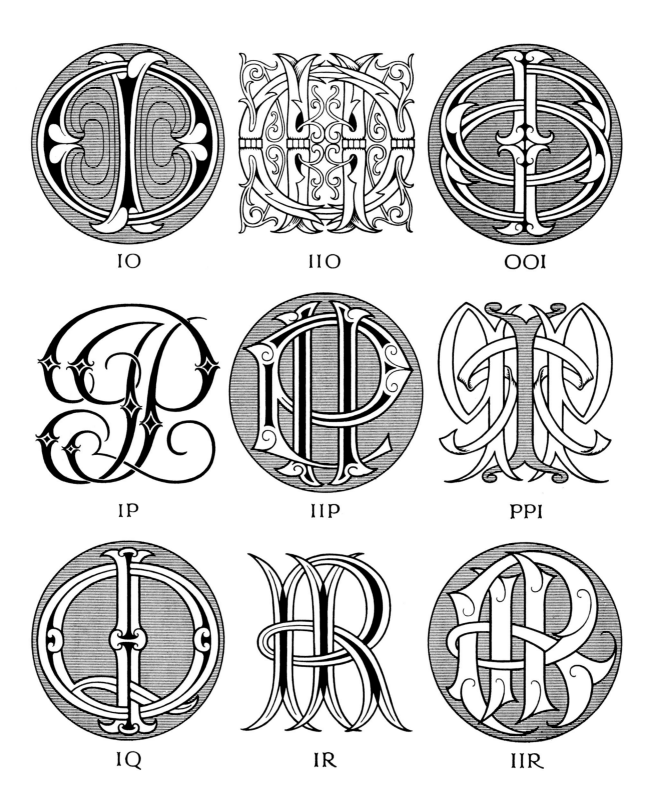

IO IIO OOI

IP IIP PPI

IQ IR IIR

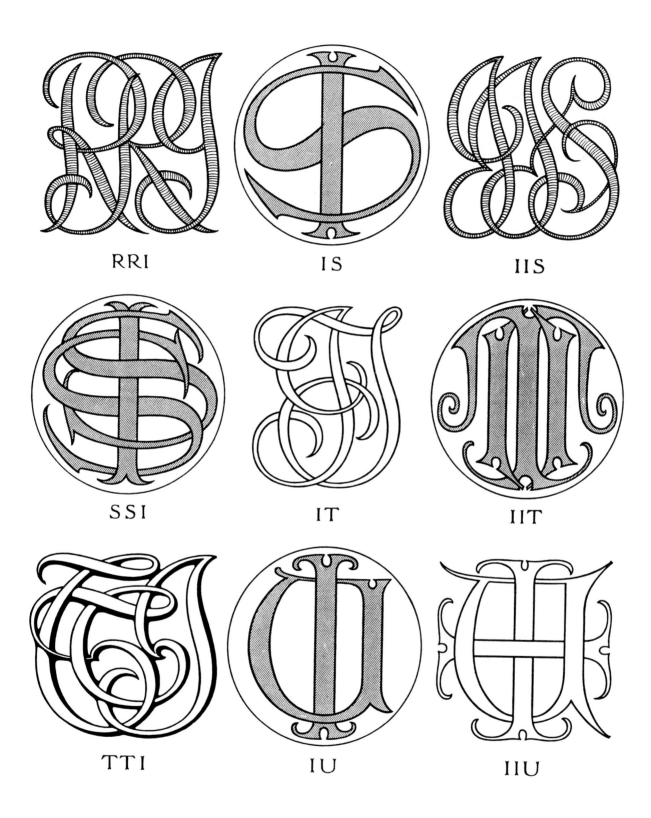

RRI

IS

IIS

SSI

IT

IIT

TTI

IU

IIU

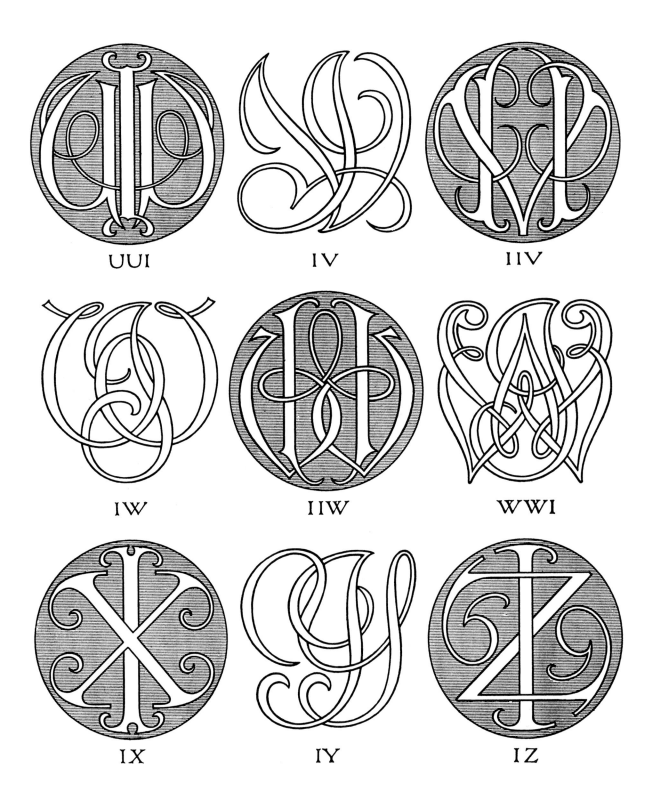

UUI       IV       IIV

IW       IIW       WWI

IX       IY       IZ

JJ       JK       JJK

KKJ       JL       LJ

JJL       LLJ       JM

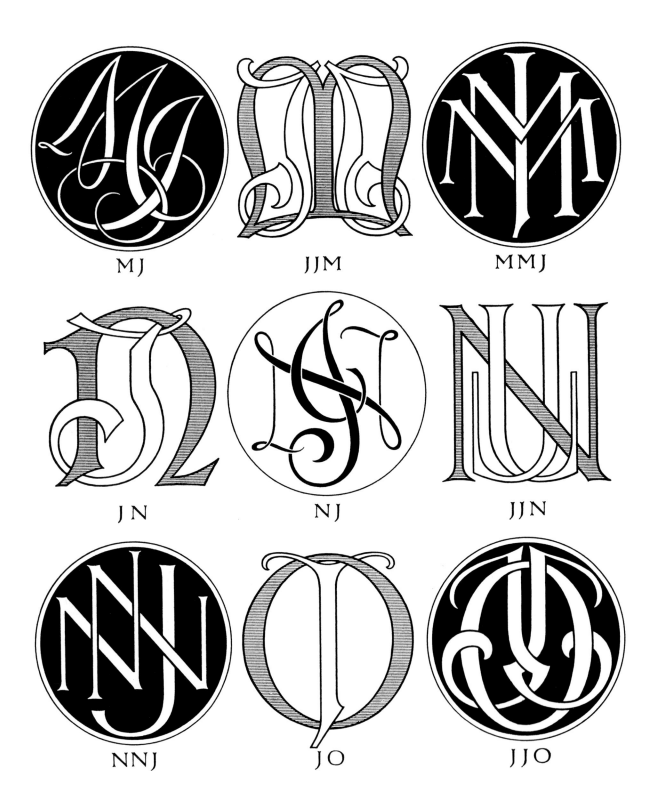

MJ

JJM

MMJ

JN

NJ

JJN

NNJ

JO

JJO

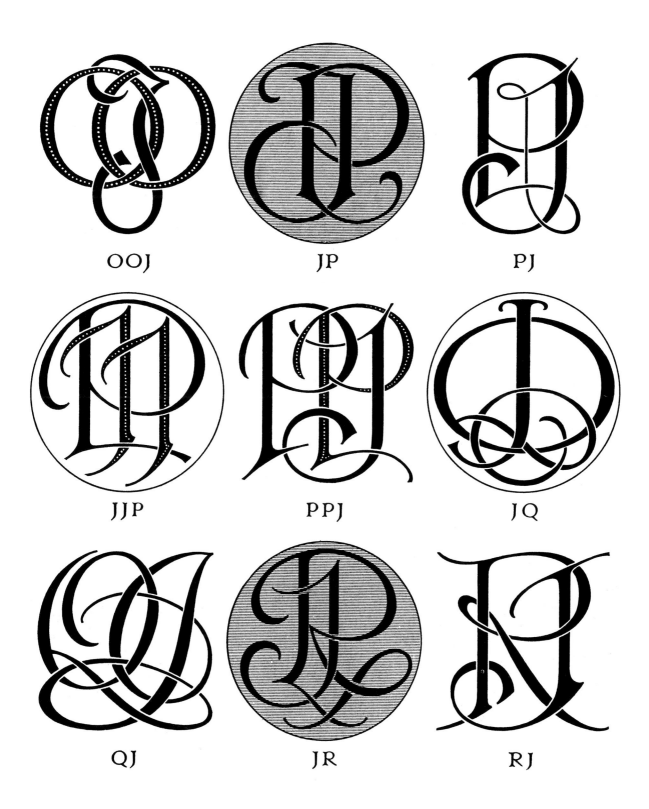

OOJ    JP    PJ

JJP    PPJ    JQ

QJ    JR    RJ

JJR   RRJ   JS

SJ   JJS   SSJ

JT   TJ   JJT

TTJ        JU        UJ

JJU        UUJ        JV

JJV        JW        WWJ

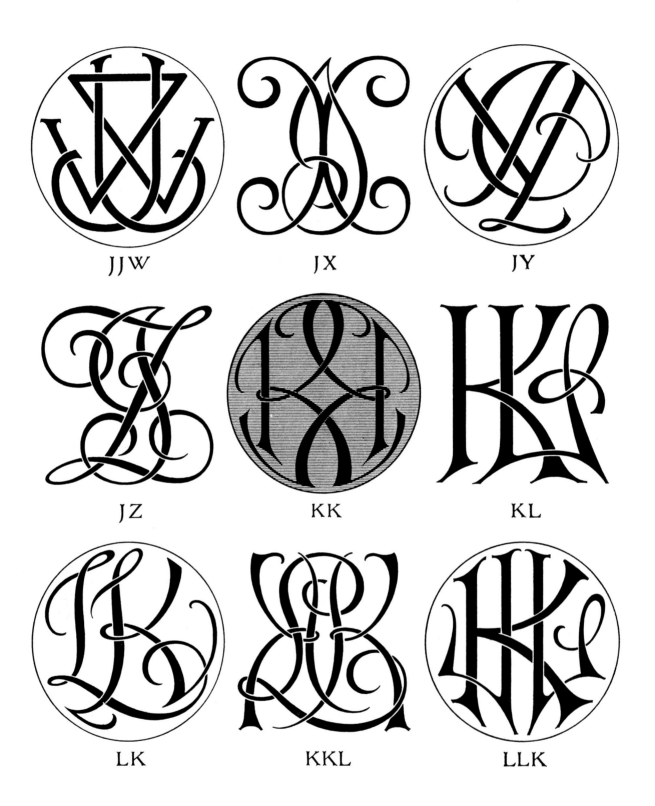

JJW  JX  JY

JZ  KK  KL

LK  KKL  LLK

166

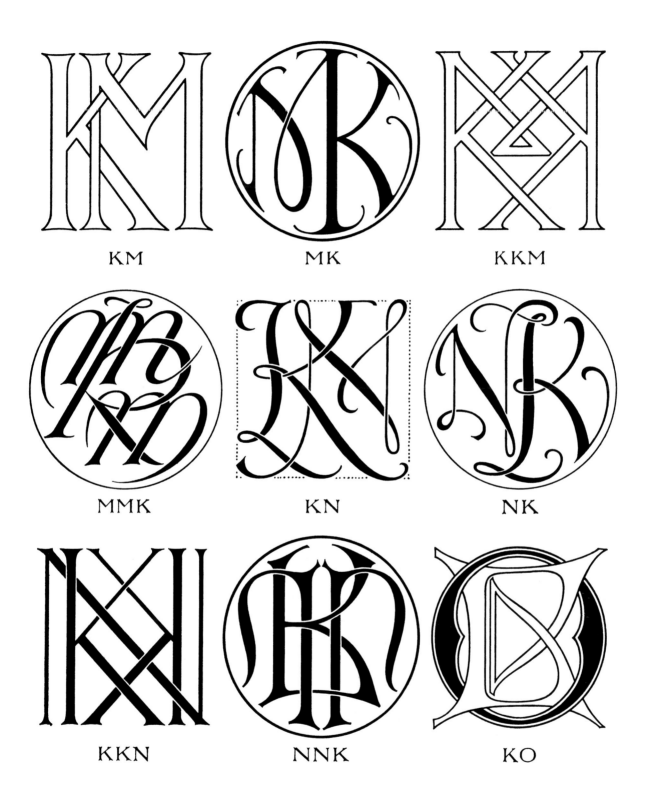

KM      MK      KKM

MMK      KN      NK

KKN      NNK      KO

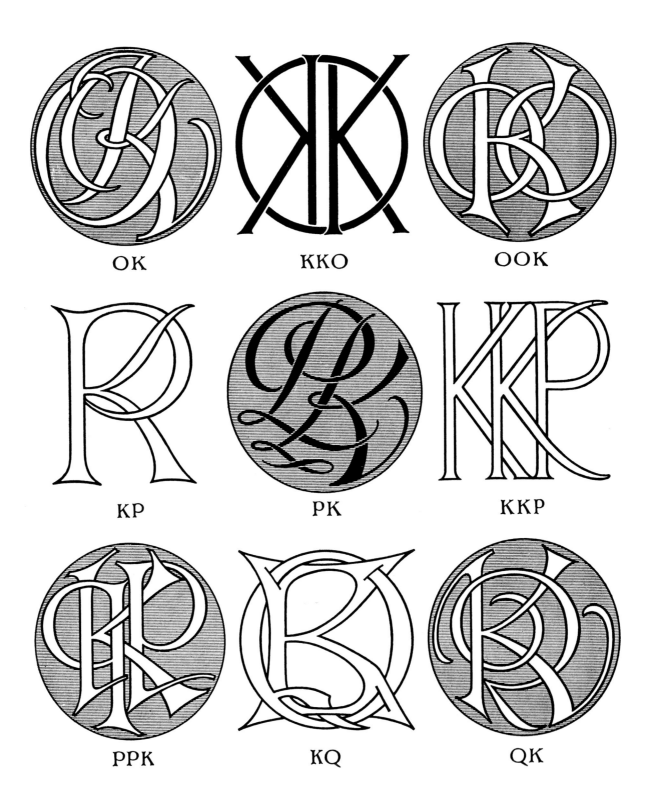

OK      KKO      OOK

KP      PK      KKP

PPK      KQ      QK

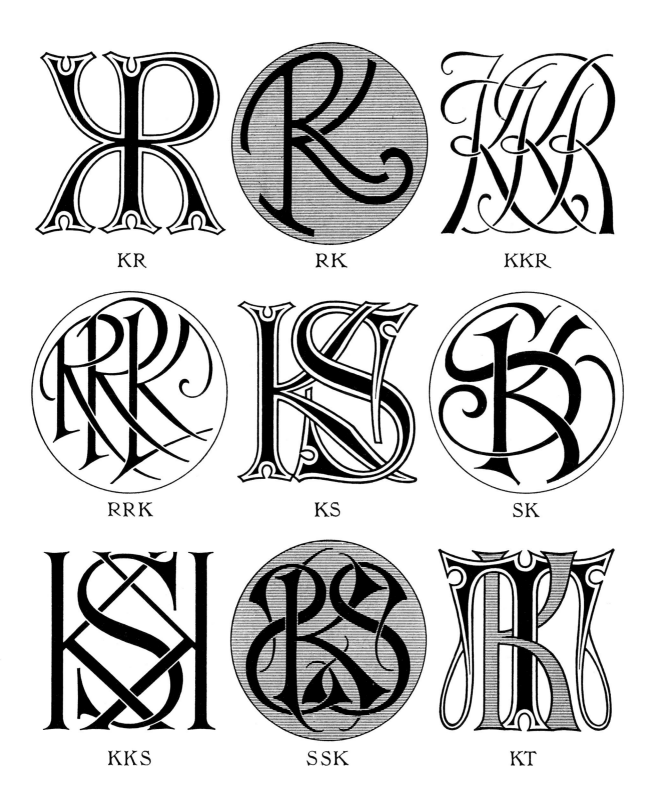

KR      RK      KKR

RRK      KS      SK

KKS      SSK      KT

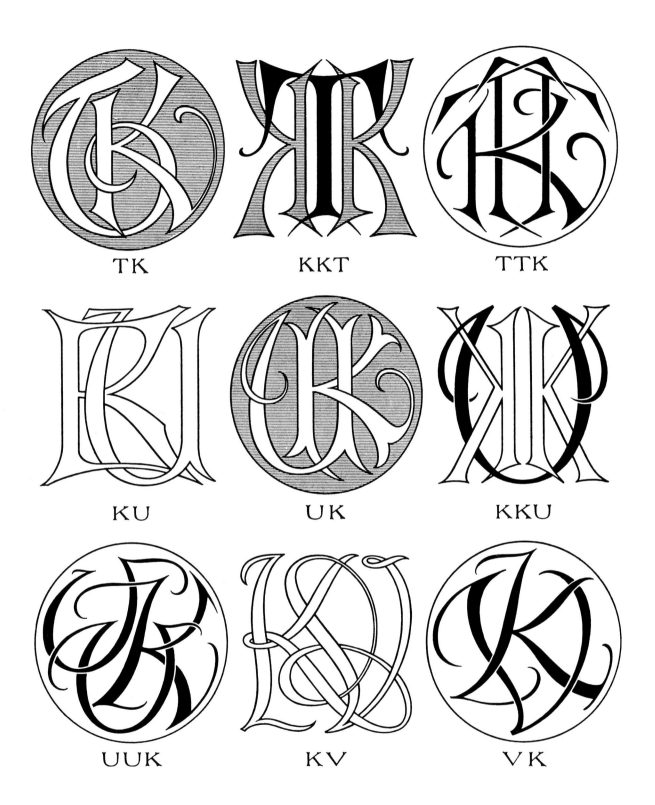

TK     KKT     TTK

KU     UK     KKU

UUK     KV     VK

KKV     KW     WK

KKW     WWK     KX

KY     KZ     ZK

LL                        LM                       ML

LLM                    MML                    LN

NL                       LLN                    NNL

LO         OL         LLO

OOL         LP         PL

LLP         LPP         LQ

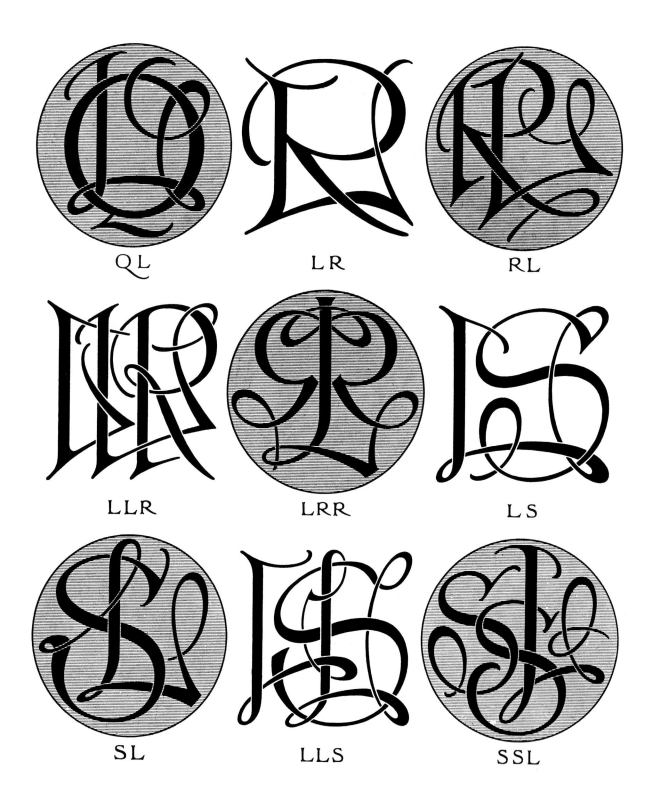

QL  LR  RL

LLR  LRR  LS

SL  LLS  SSL

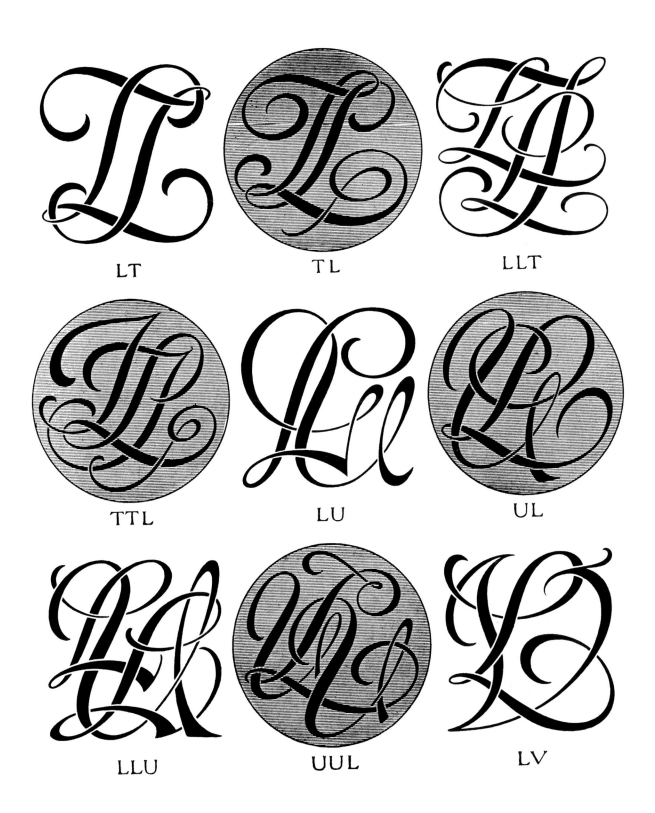

LT    TL    LLT

TTL    LU    UL

LLU    UUL    LV

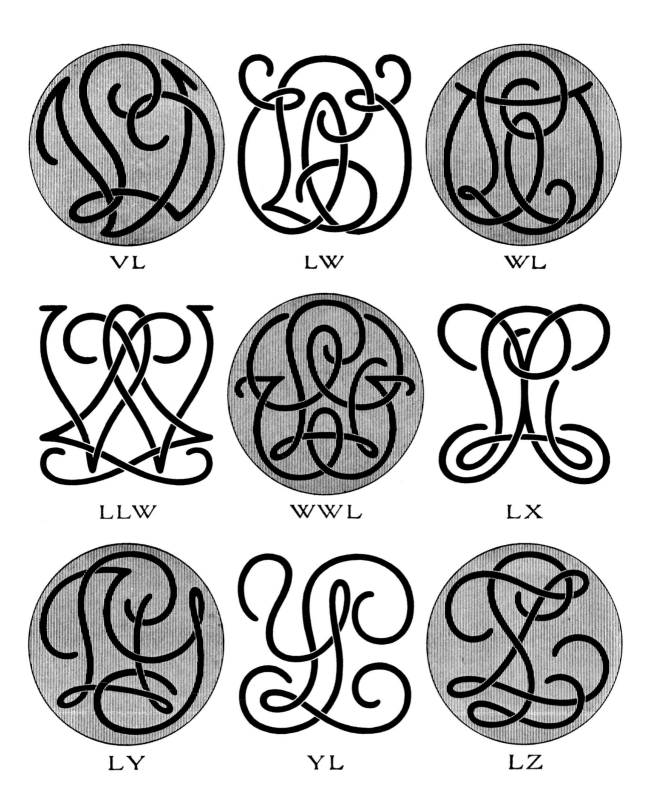

VL  LW  WL

LLW  WWL  LX

LY  YL  LZ

MM      MN      NM

MMN      NMN      MO

OM      MMO      OOM

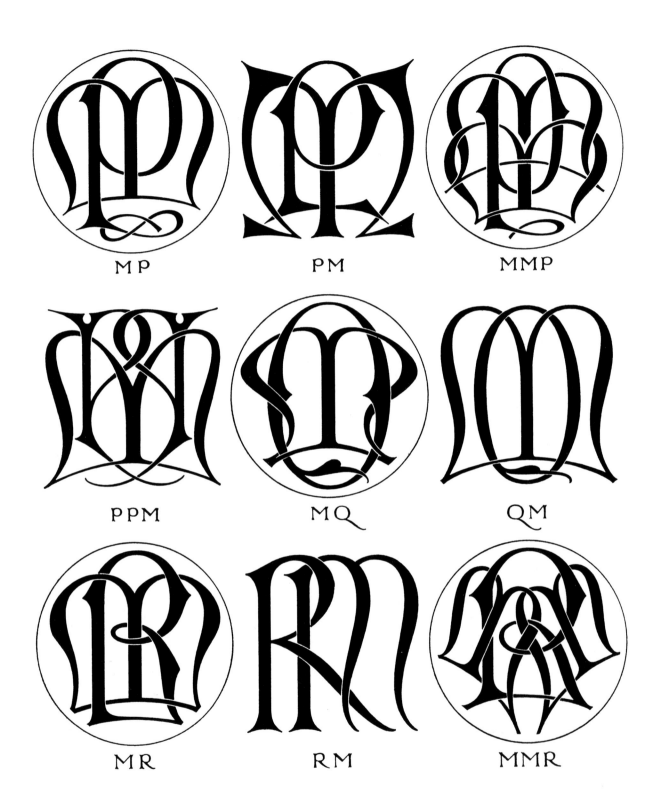

MP     PM     MMP

PPM     MQ     QM

MR     RM     MMR

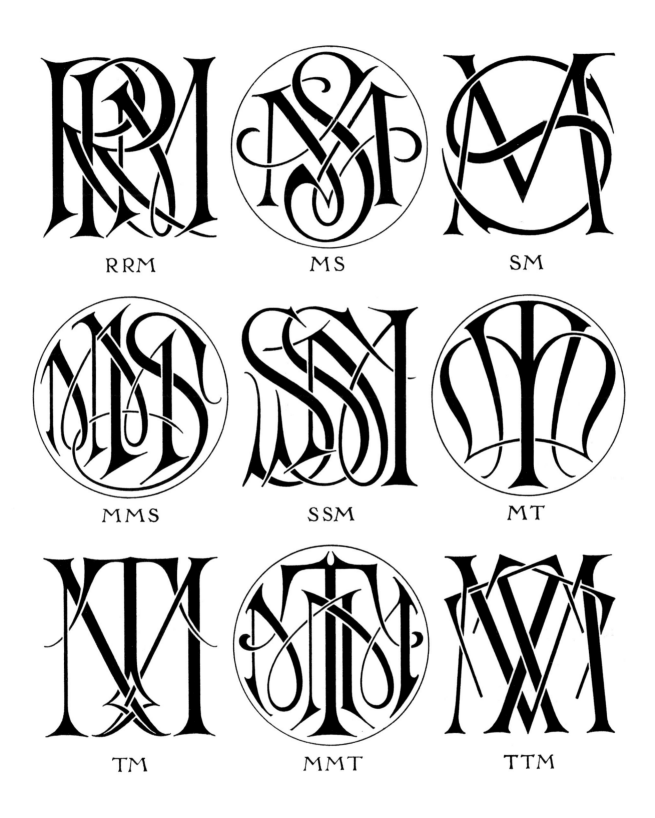

RRM     MS     SM

MMS     SSM     MT

TM     MMT     TTM

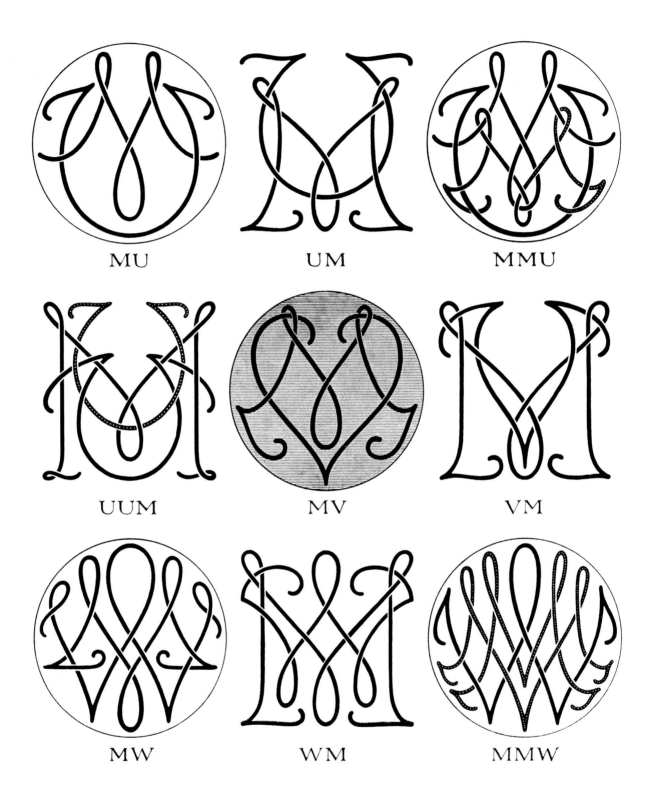

MU          UM          MMU

UUM          MV          VM

MW          WM          MMW

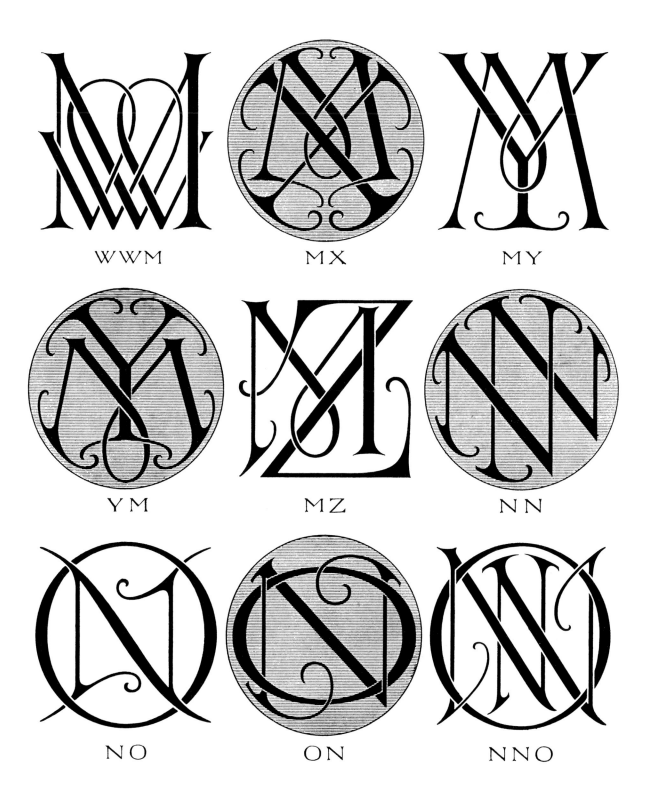

WWM     MX     MY

YM     MZ     NN

NO     ON     NNO

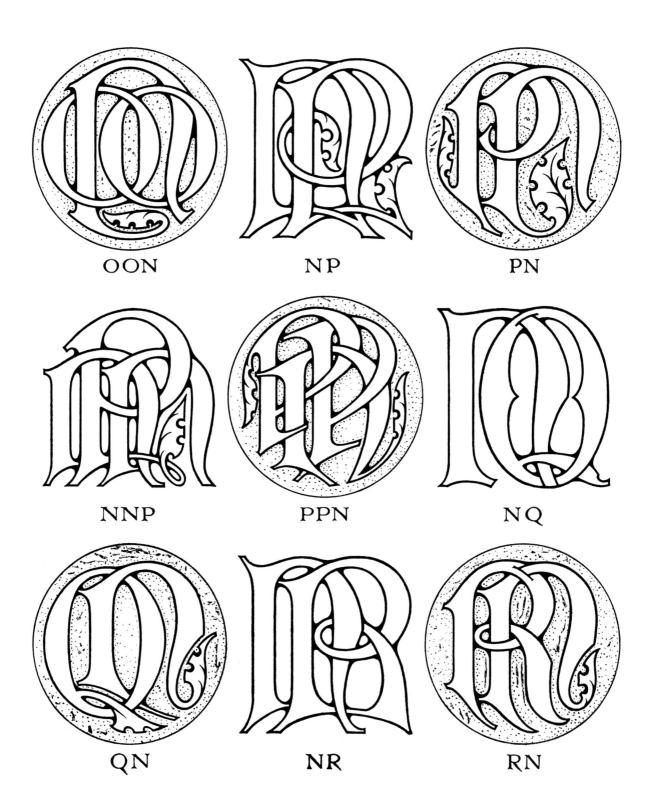

OON  NP  PN

NNP  PPN  NQ

QN  NR  RN

NNR · RRN · N S

S N · NNS · S SN

N T · T N · NNT

TTN      NU      UN

NNU      UUN      NV

VN      NW      WN

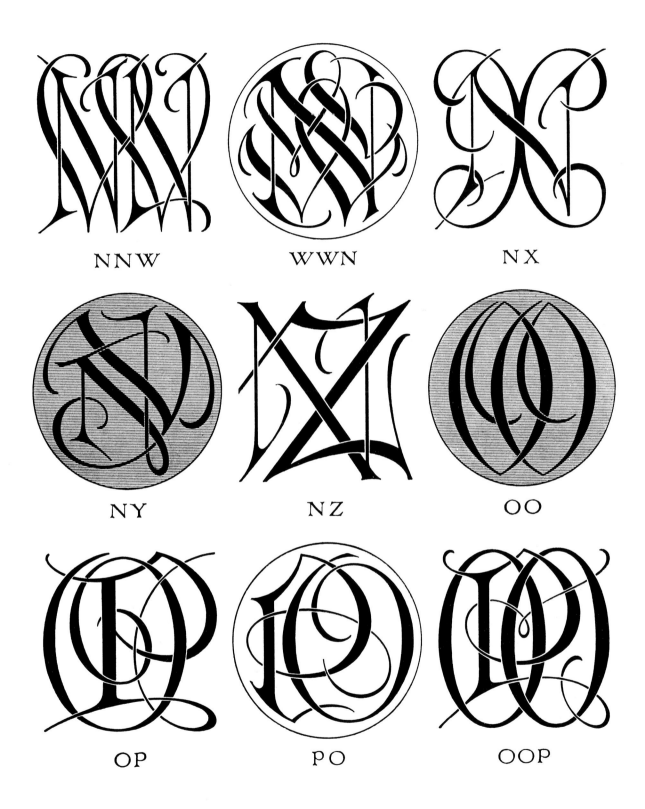

NNW  WWN  NX

NY  NZ  OO

OP  PO  OOP

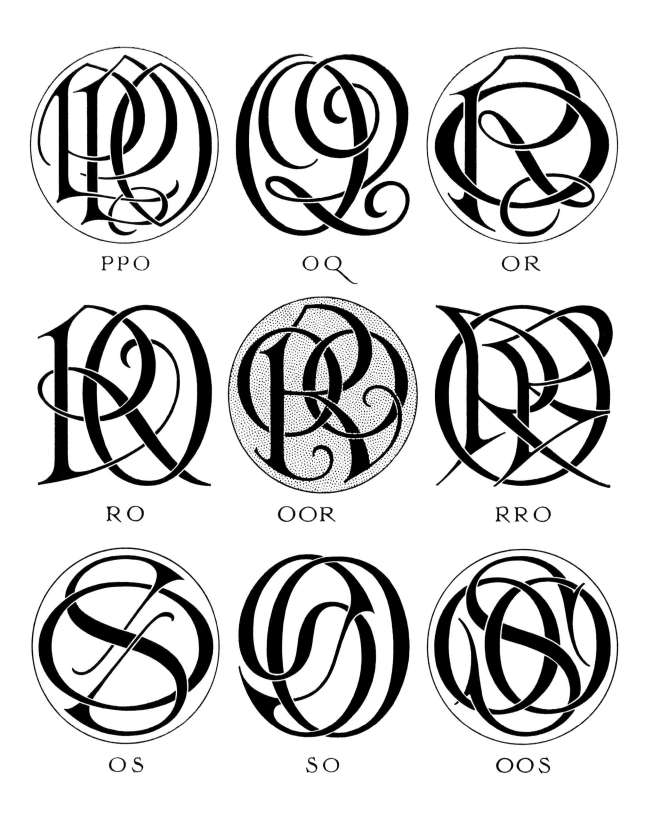

PPO        OQ        OR

RO        OOR        RRO

OS        SO        OOS

SSO      OT      TO

OOT      TTO      OU

UO      OV      VO

OOV      VVO      OW

WO      OOW      WWO

OX      OY      OZ

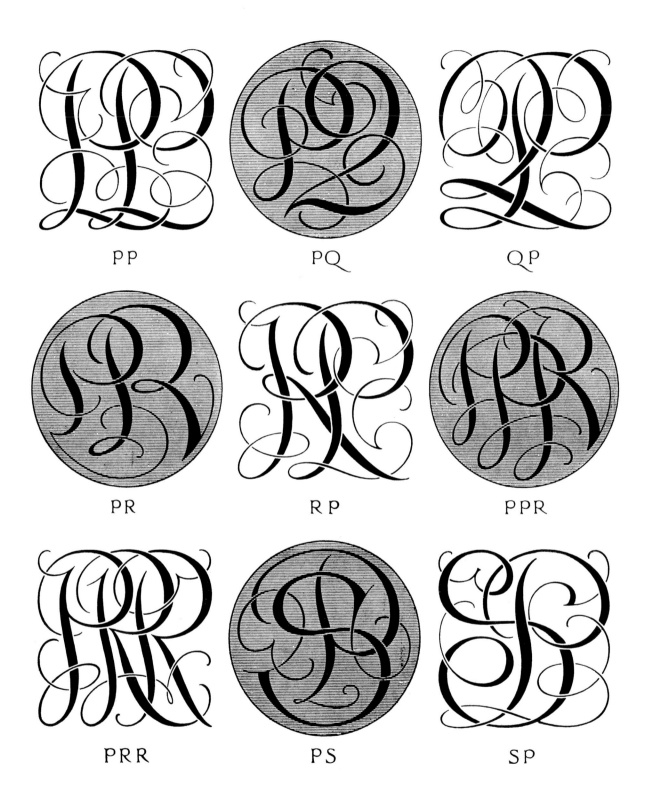

PP          PQ          QP

PR          RP          PPR

PRR         PS          SP

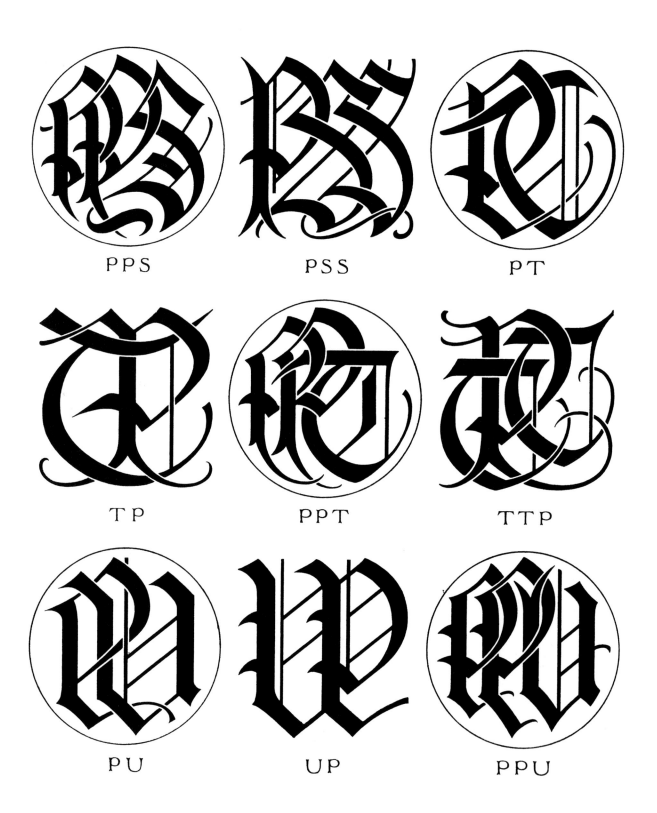

PPS       PSS       PT

TP       PPT       TTP

PU       UP       PPU

UUP            PV            VP

ppv            pw            WP

ppw            WWP            PX

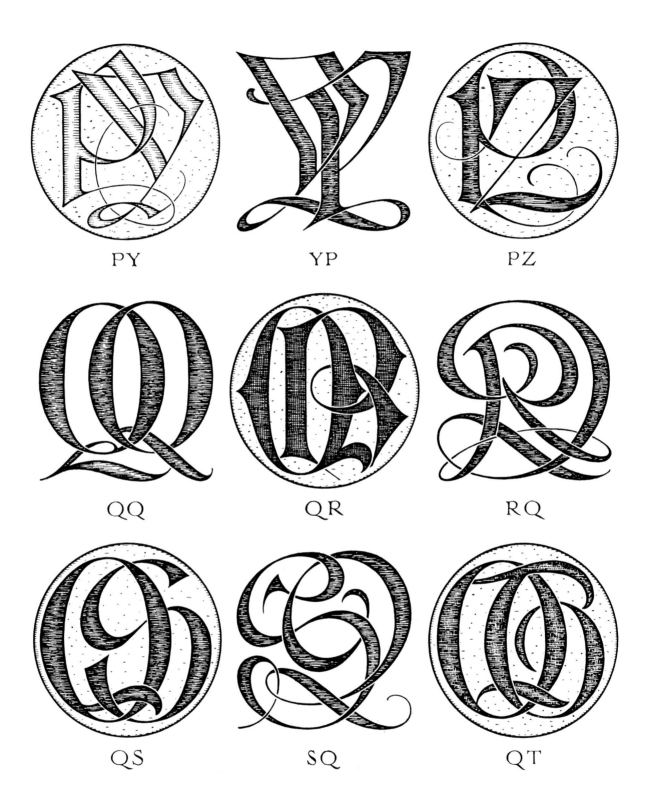

PY          YP          PZ

QQ          QR          RQ

QS          SQ          QT

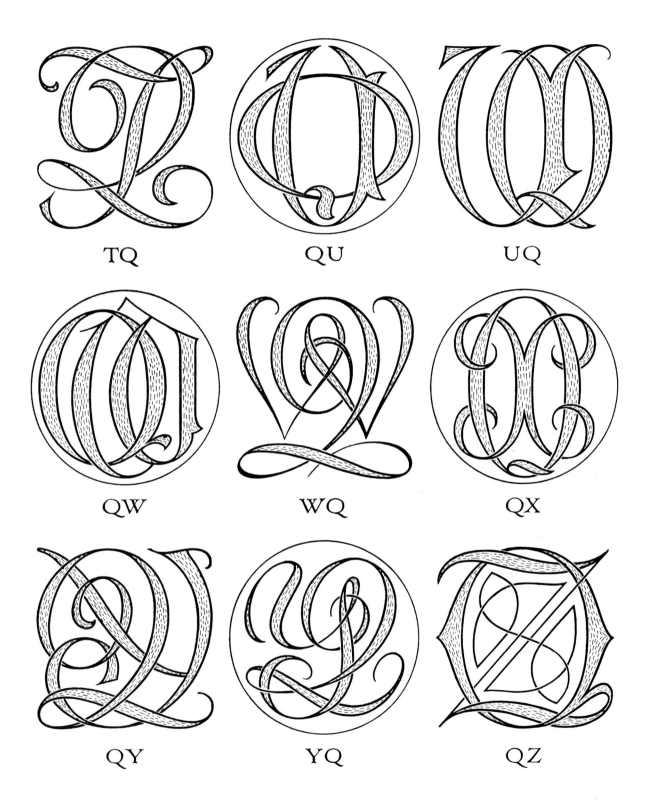

TQ          QU          UQ

QW          WQ          QX

QY          YQ          QZ

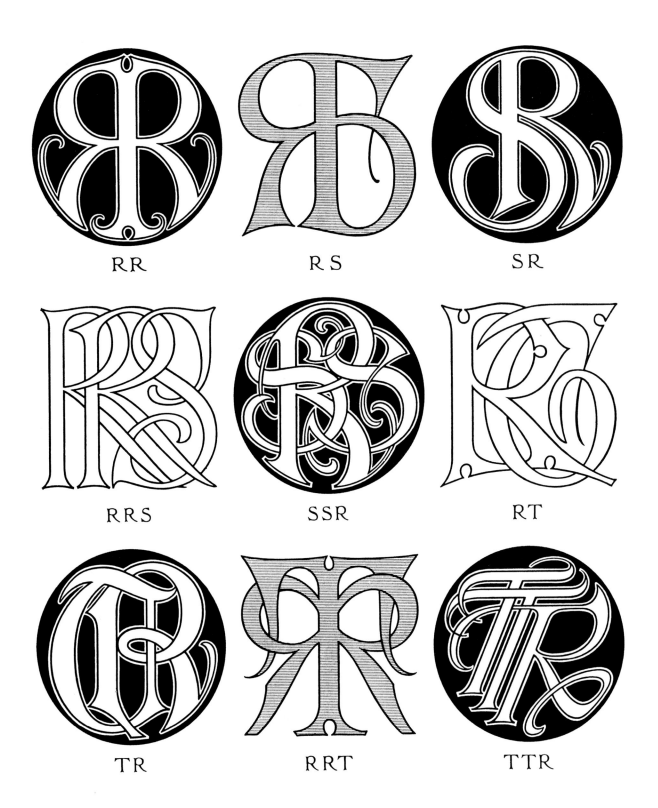

RR      RS      SR

RRS      SSR      RT

TR      RRT      TTR

RU  UR  RRU

UUR  RV  VR

RW  WR  RRW

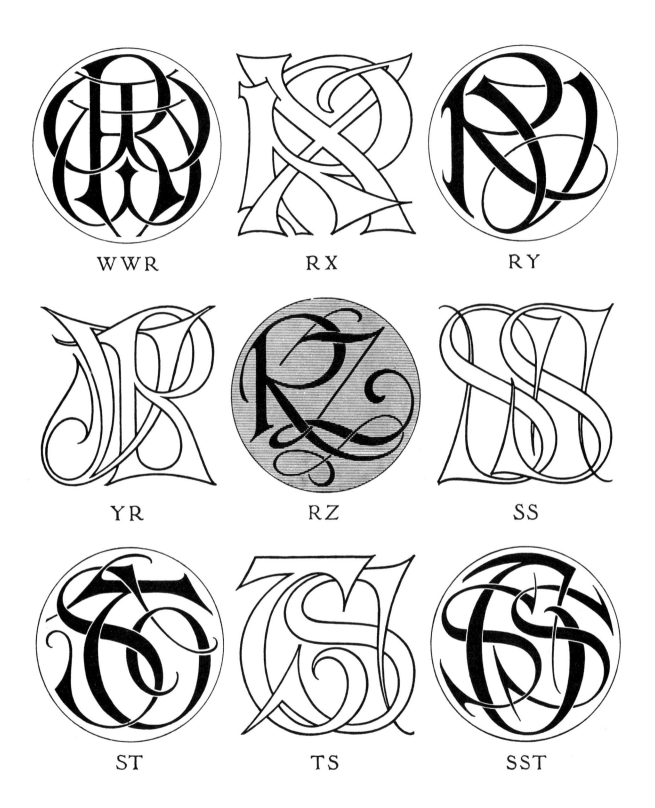

WWR      RX      RY

YR      RZ      SS

ST      TS      SST

TTS     SU     US

USS     SV     VS

SSV     SW     WS

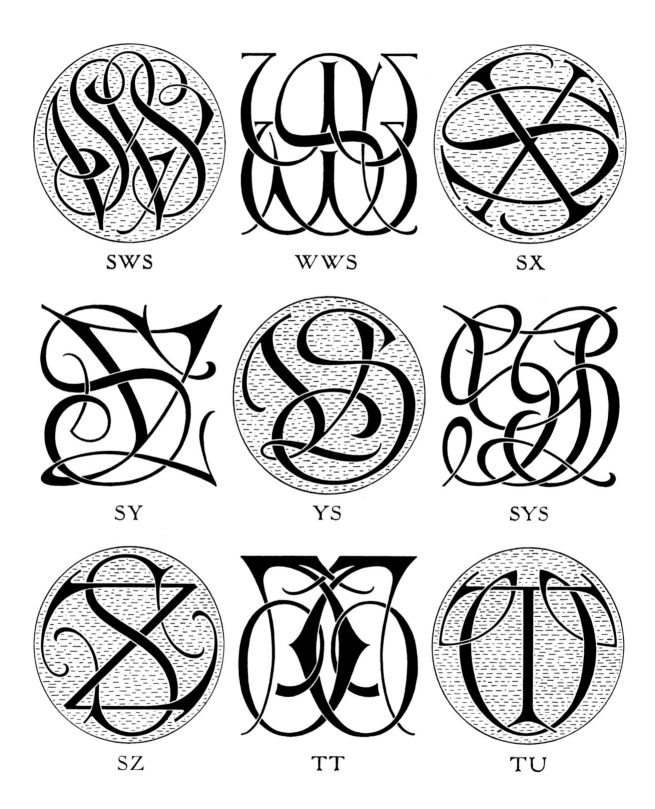

SWS     WWS     SX

SY     YS     SYS

SZ     TT     TU

UT     TTU     UUT

TV     VT     TTV

TW     WT     TTW

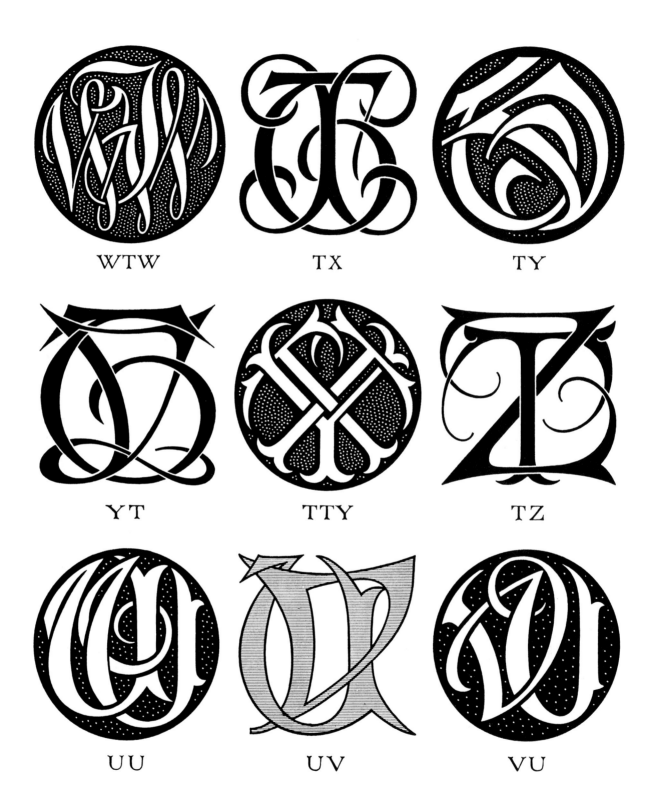

WTW       TX       TY

YT       TTY       TZ

UU       UV       VU

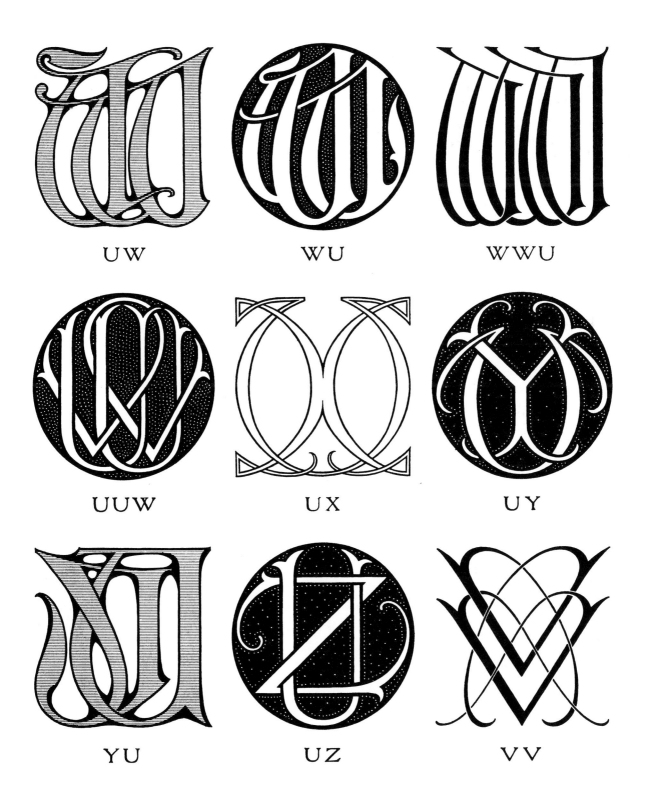

UW WU WWU

UUW UX UY

YU UZ VV

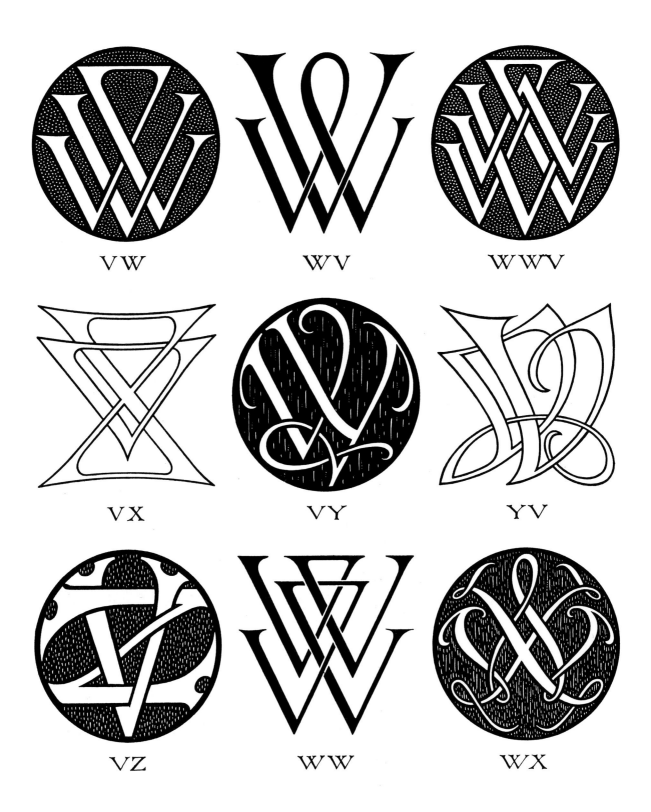

VW      WV      WWV

VX      VY      YV

VZ      WW      WX

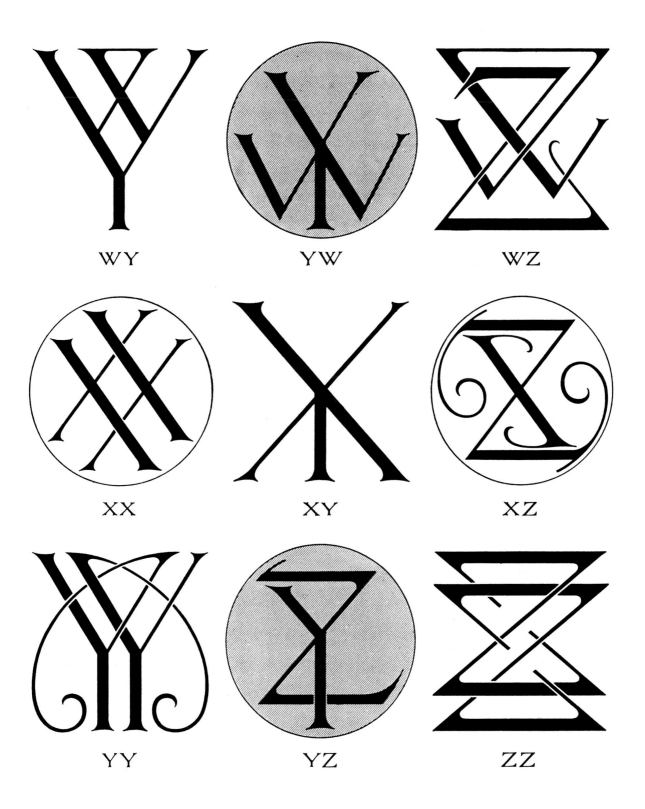

WY      YW      WZ

XX      XY      XZ

YY      YZ      ZZ

ABC BCD CDE

DEF EFG FGH

GHI HIJ IJK

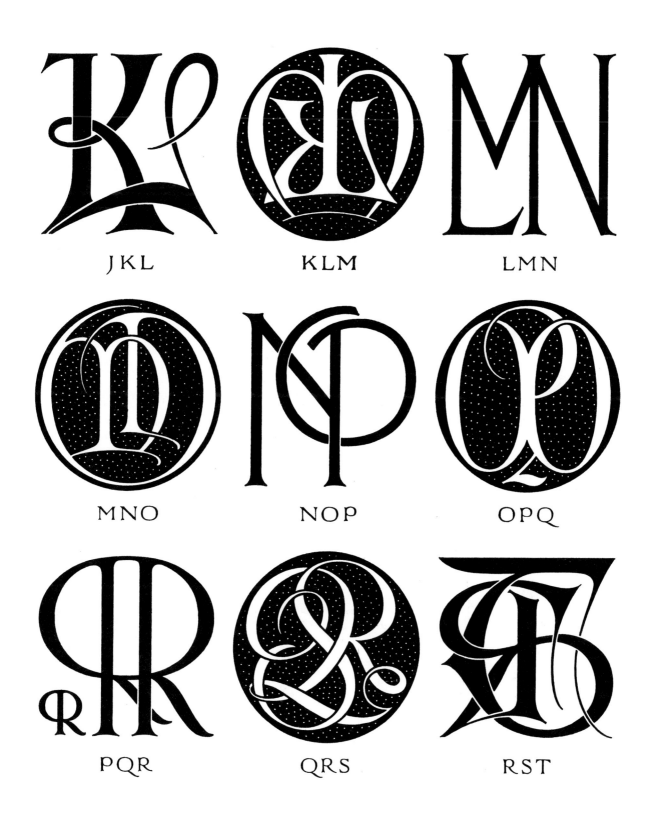

JKL       KLM       LMN

MNO       NOP       OPQ

PQR       QRS       RST

STU  STU  TUV

TUV  UVW  UVW

VWX  WXY  XYZ

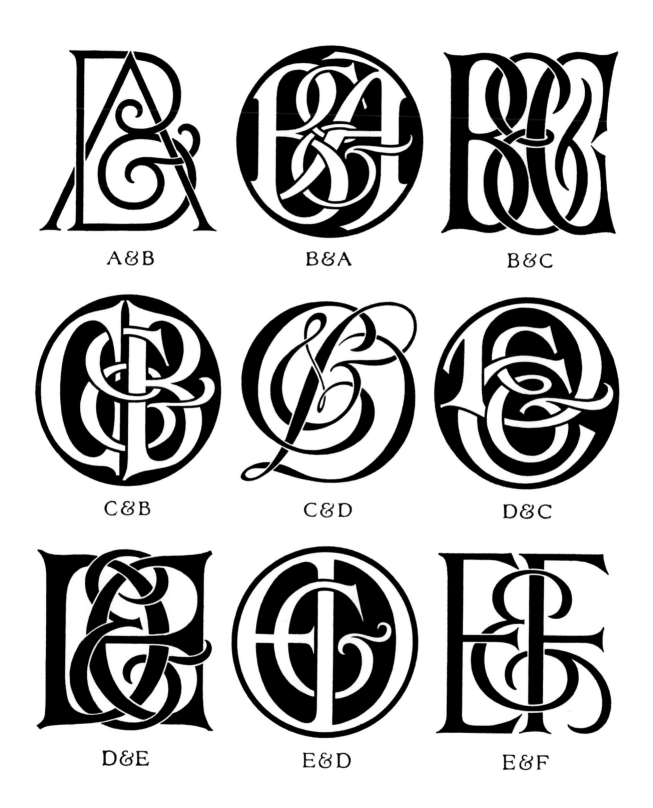

A&B  B&A  B&C

C&B  C&D  D&C

D&E  E&D  E&F

F&E         F&G         G&F

G&H         H&G         H&I

I&H         I&J         J&K

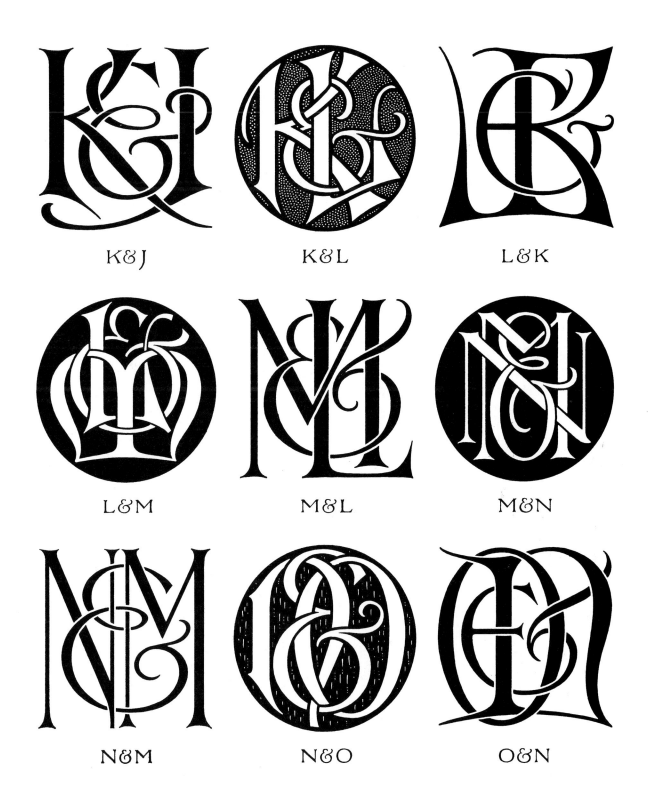

K&J       K&L       L&K

L&M       M&L       M&N

N&M       N&O       O&N

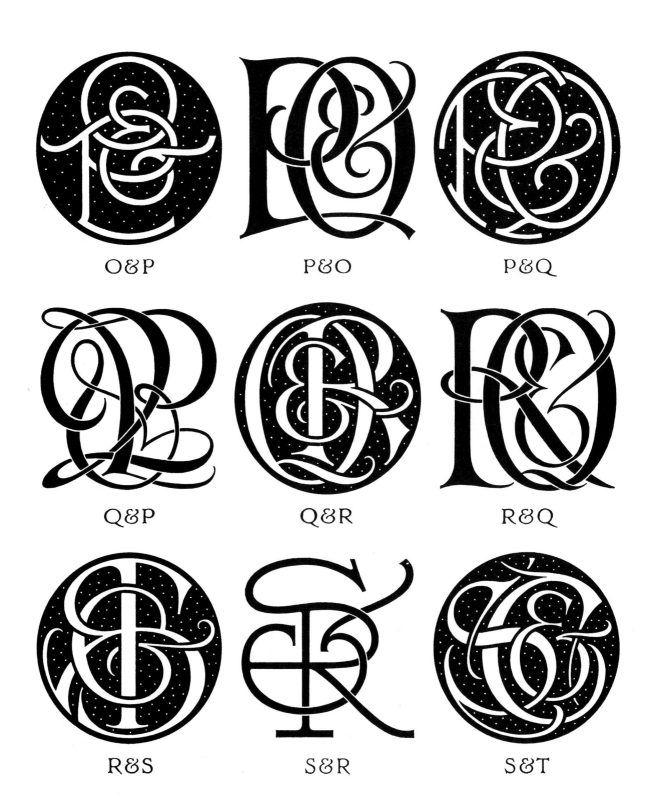

| O&P | P&O | P&Q |
|-----|-----|-----|
| Q&P | Q&R | R&Q |
| R&S | S&R | S&T |

210

T & S    T & U    U & T

U & V    V & U    V & W

W & V    W & X    Y & Z

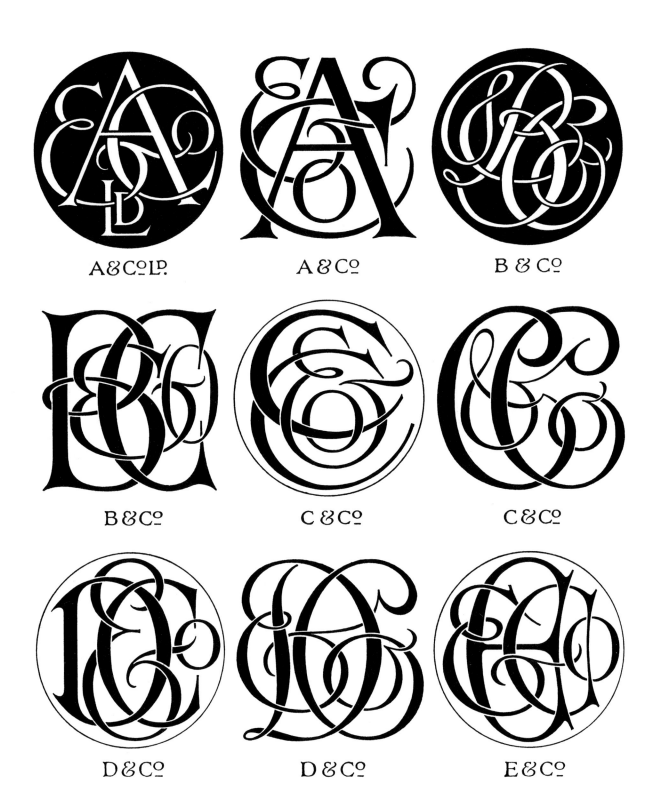

A & Cᵒ Lᴰ.          A & Cᵒ          B & Cᵒ

B & Cᵒ          C & Cᵒ          C & Cᵒ

D & Cᵒ          D & Cᵒ          E & Cᵒ

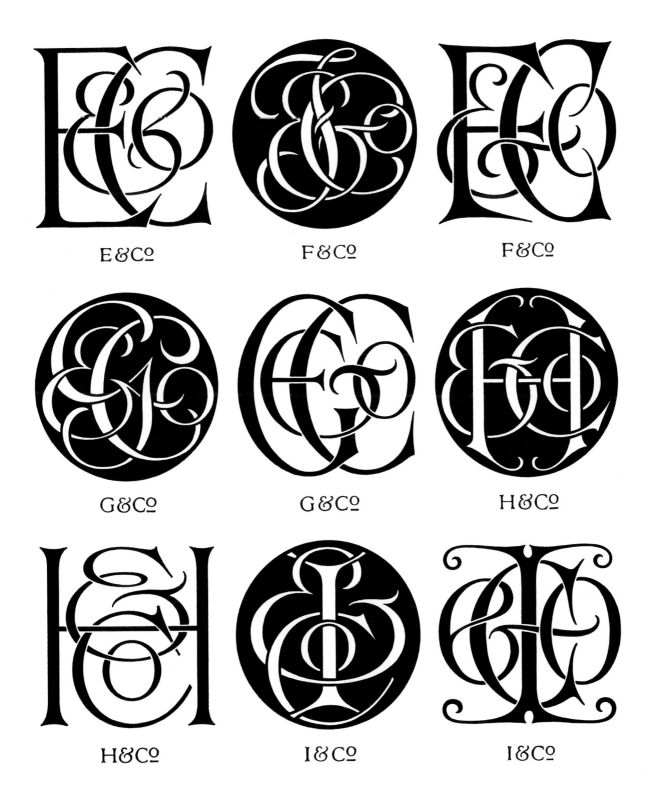

E&C̲ꝋ       F&C̲ꝋ       F&C̲ꝋ

G&C̲ꝋ       G&C̲ꝋ       H&C̲ꝋ

H&C̲ꝋ       I&C̲ꝋ       I&C̲ꝋ

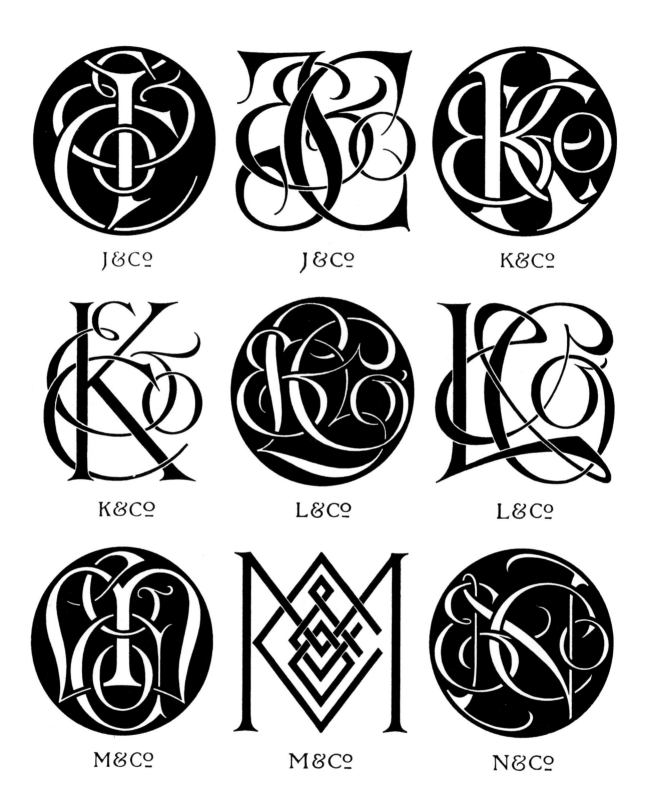

J&Cọ  J&Cọ  K&Cọ

K&Cọ  L&Cọ  L&Cọ

M&Cọ  M&Cọ  N&Cọ

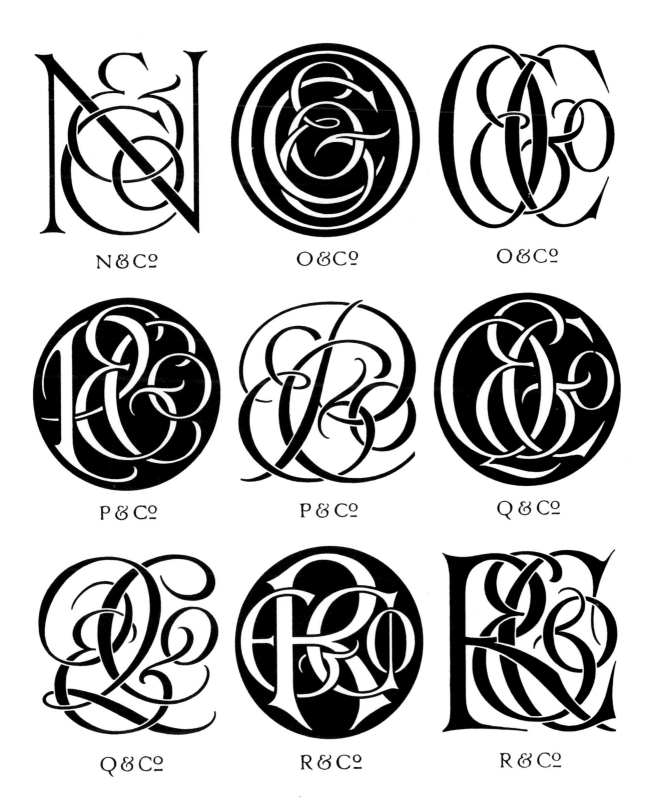

N & Cº       O & Cº       O & Cº

P & Cº       P & Cº       Q & Cº

Q & Cº       R & Cº       R & Cº

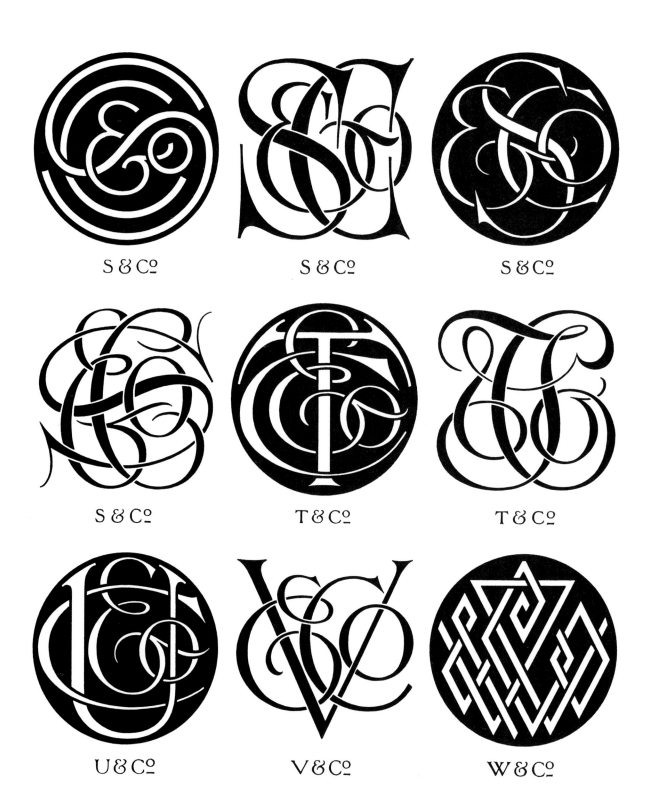

S & Cº       S & Cº       S & Cº

S & Cº       T & Cº       T & Cº

U & Cº       V & Cº       W & Cº

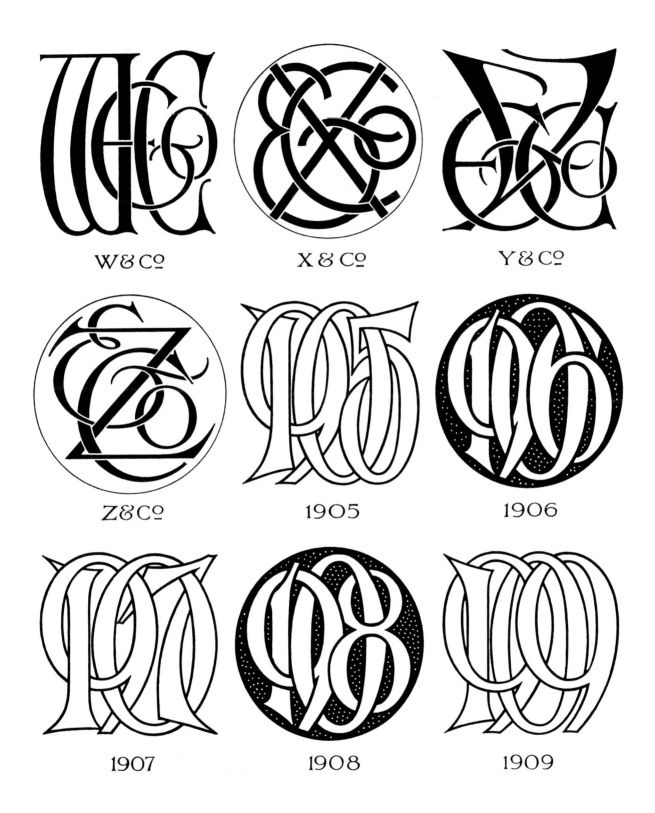

W & Co

X & Co

Y & Co

Z & Co

1905

1906

1907

1908

1909

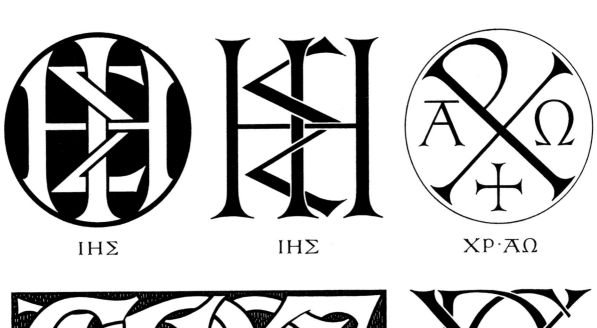

IHΣ        IHΣ        XP·ĀΩ

CHRIST        XPC

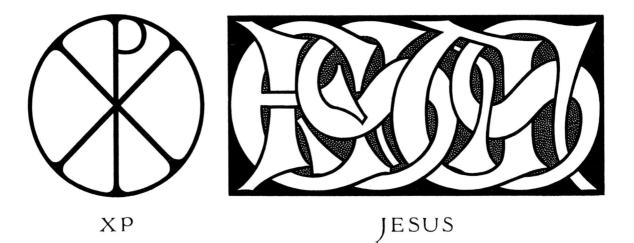

XP        JESUS

MARY

XPΣ

XPC

JOSEPH

INRI

IHS

AΩ  INRI

ALPHA  AΩ

AΩ  OMEGA

IHS          IHS          IHS

XPC          IHC          IHC

IHC          IHS          XPS

221

ANNO

AD

AD

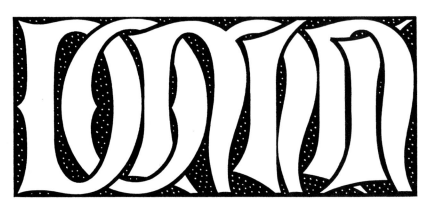

DOMINI

AD

AD

AD

JRL

OWH

GGB

DGR

FWF

JGW

EAP

RWE

HWL

JRG

SAB

AWP

JAF

LFA

JFC

EBB

CLORIA·N·EX-
CELSIS·DO·LAS
EO·Ƥ·ANO
DOMIN·ᵫDOS
DO·VOLENE·V

LHK

OGS

HD

MC

KW

MHT

AR

OH

AP

CGE

P. S.

VK

CP

LOU

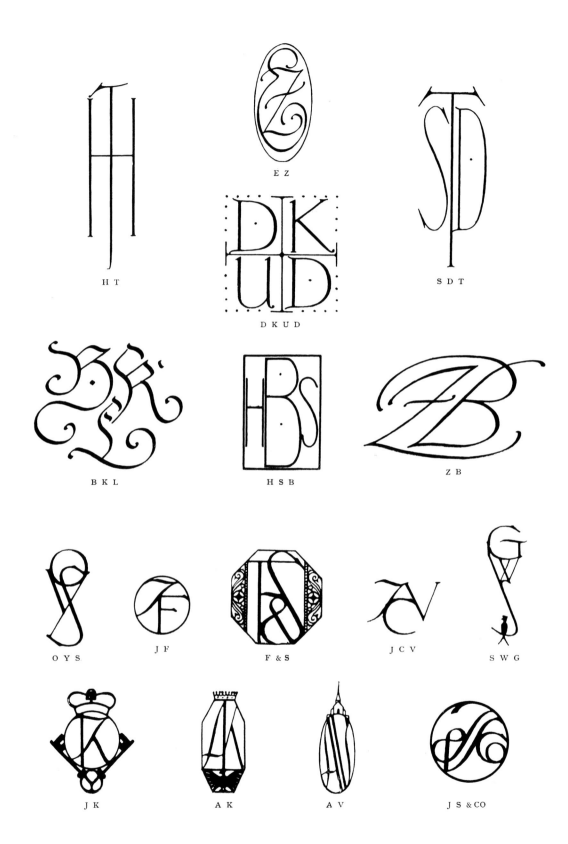

EZ

HT

DKUD

SDT

BKL

HSB

ZB

OYS

JF

F & S

JCV

SWG

JK

AK

AV

JS & CO

T W

W

W ST F A K

O Z

E R

K E

J B

M K

E K J

RN  ᴴ

W
T  ᴴᴷ

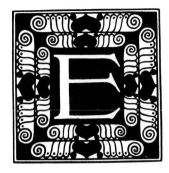  

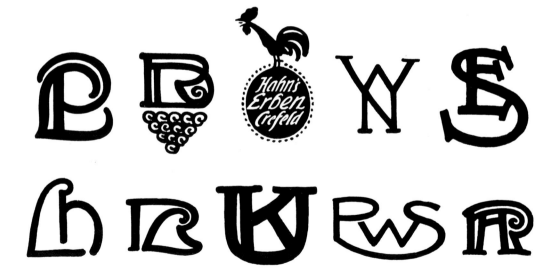

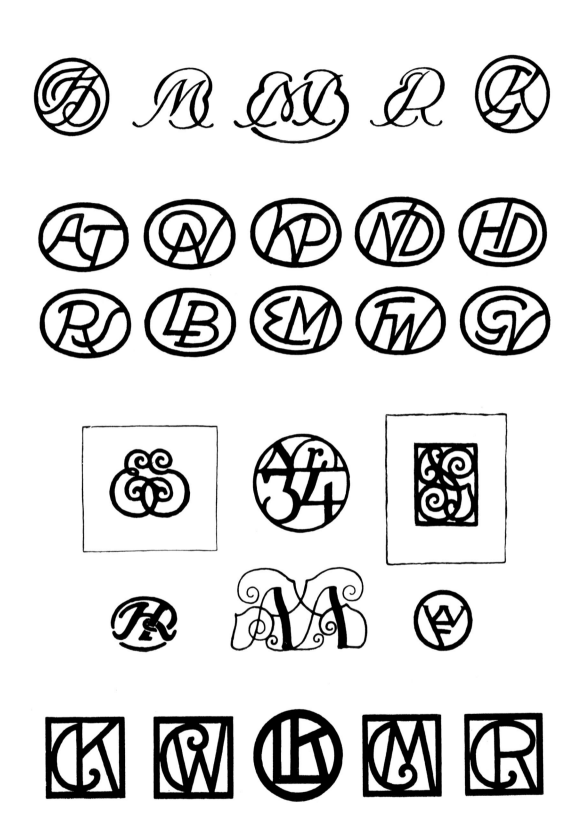

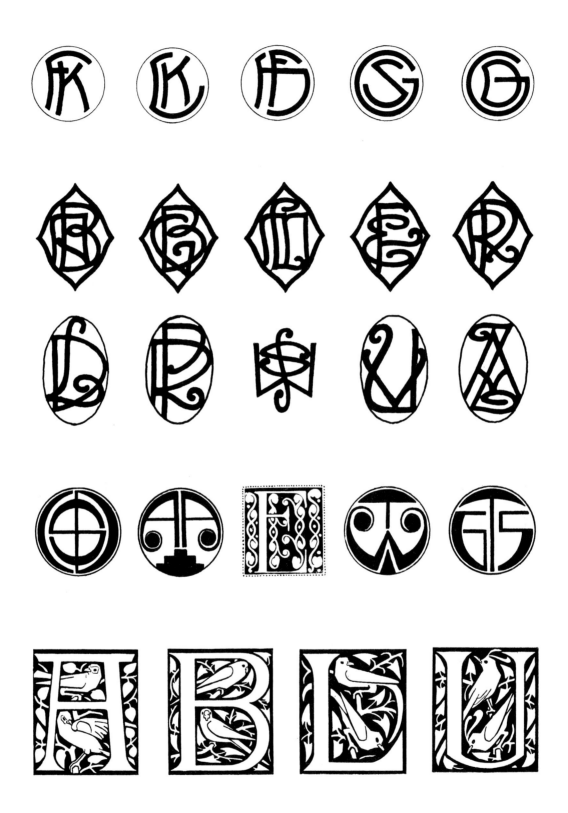

240

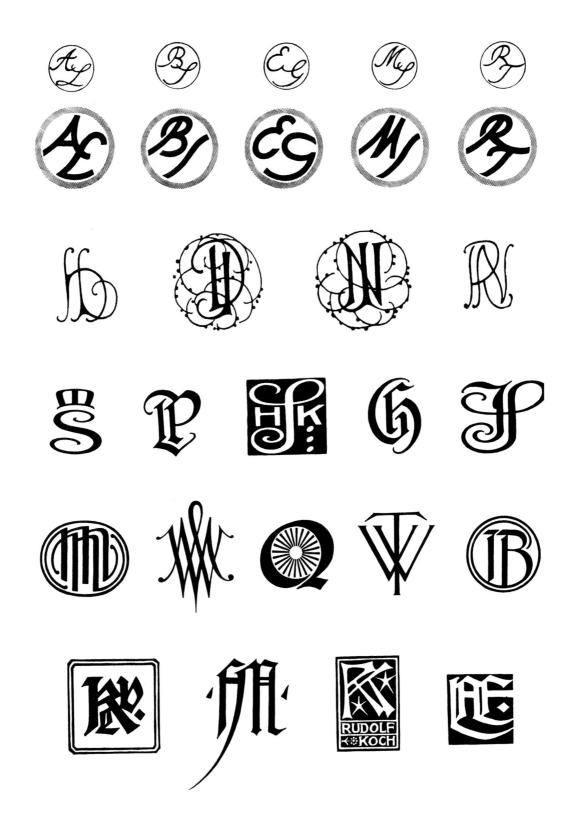

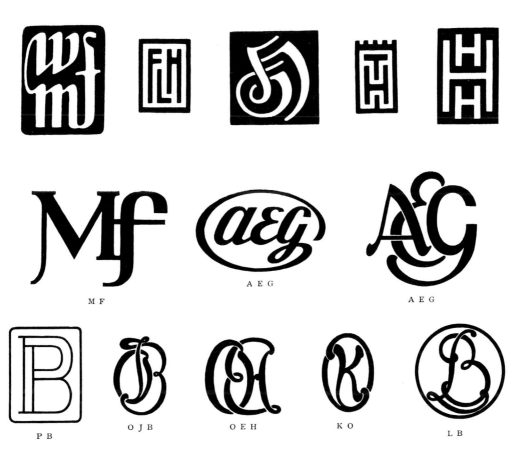

MF

A E G

A E G

P B     O J B     O E H     K O     L B

O M C     N G     S K     A H O     R K

245

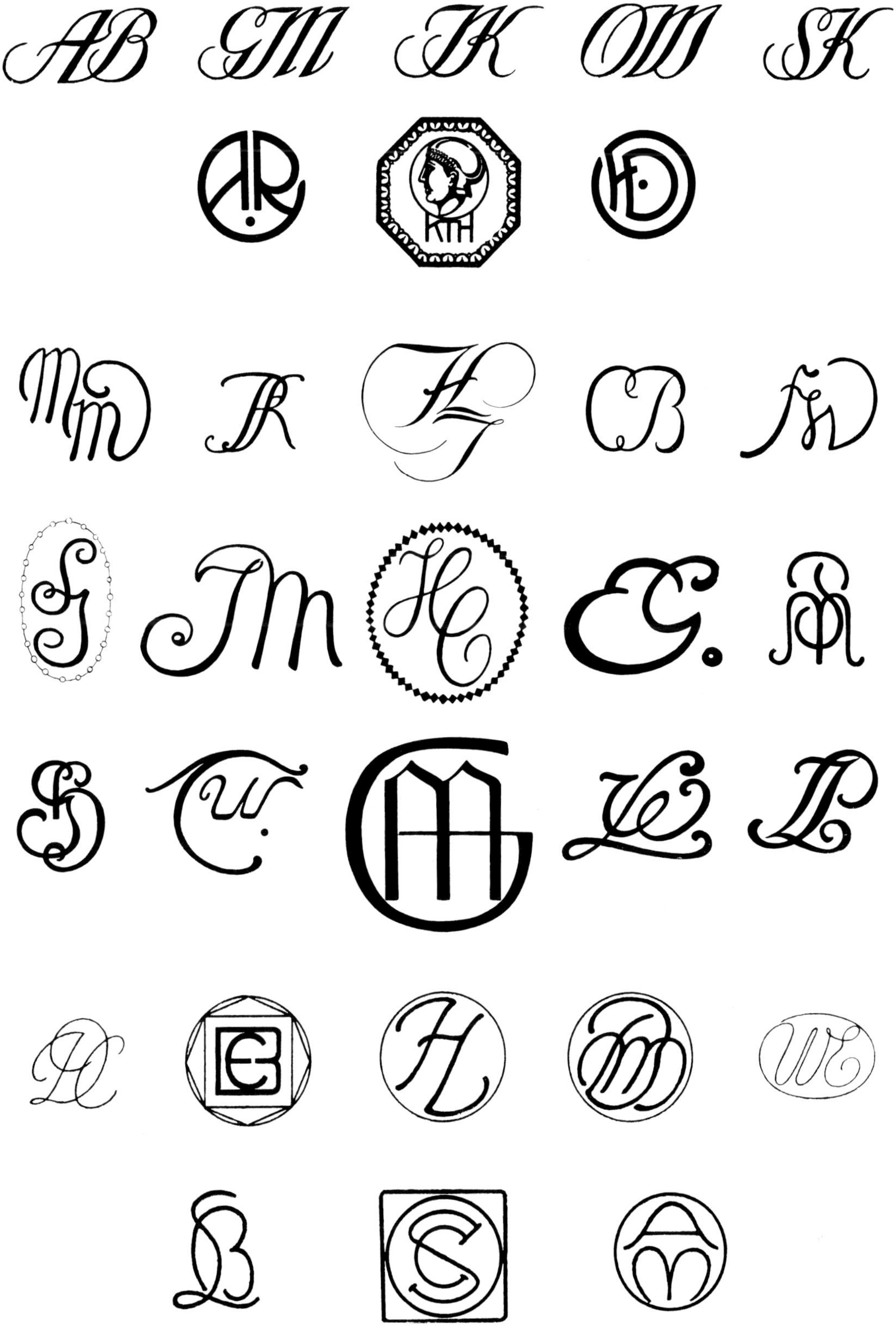

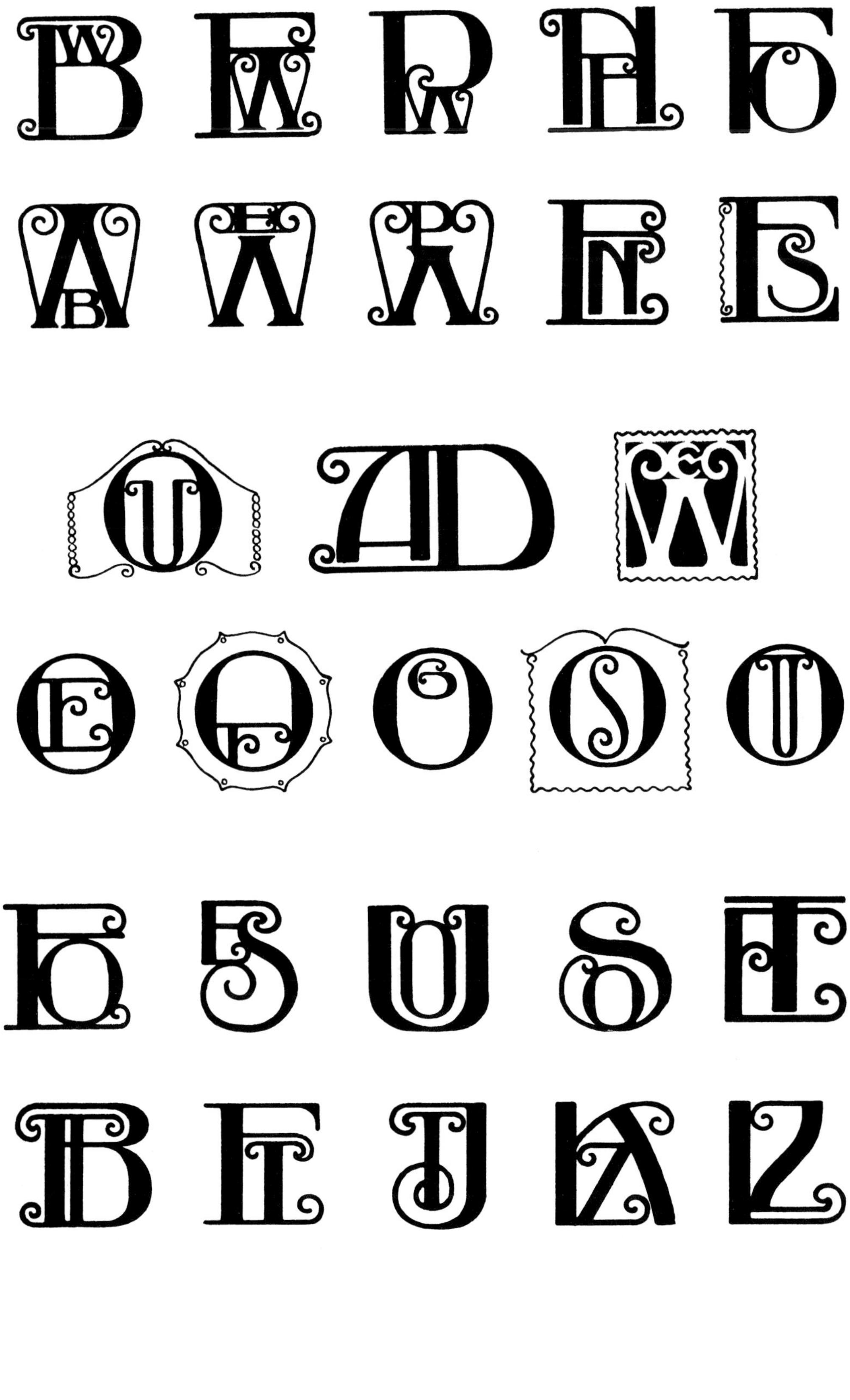

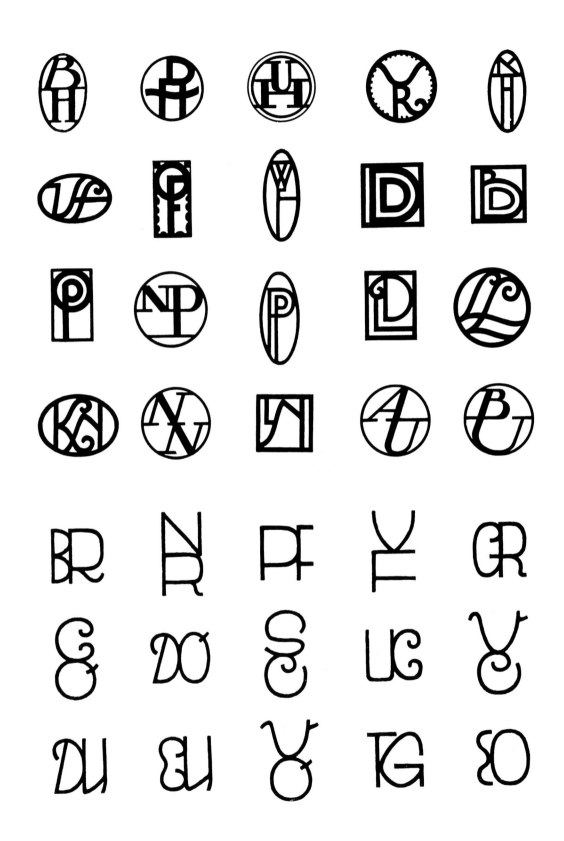

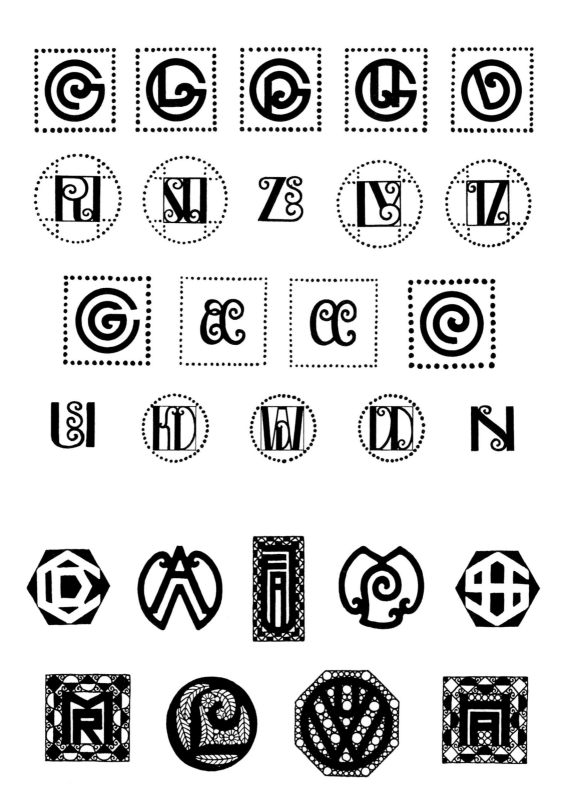

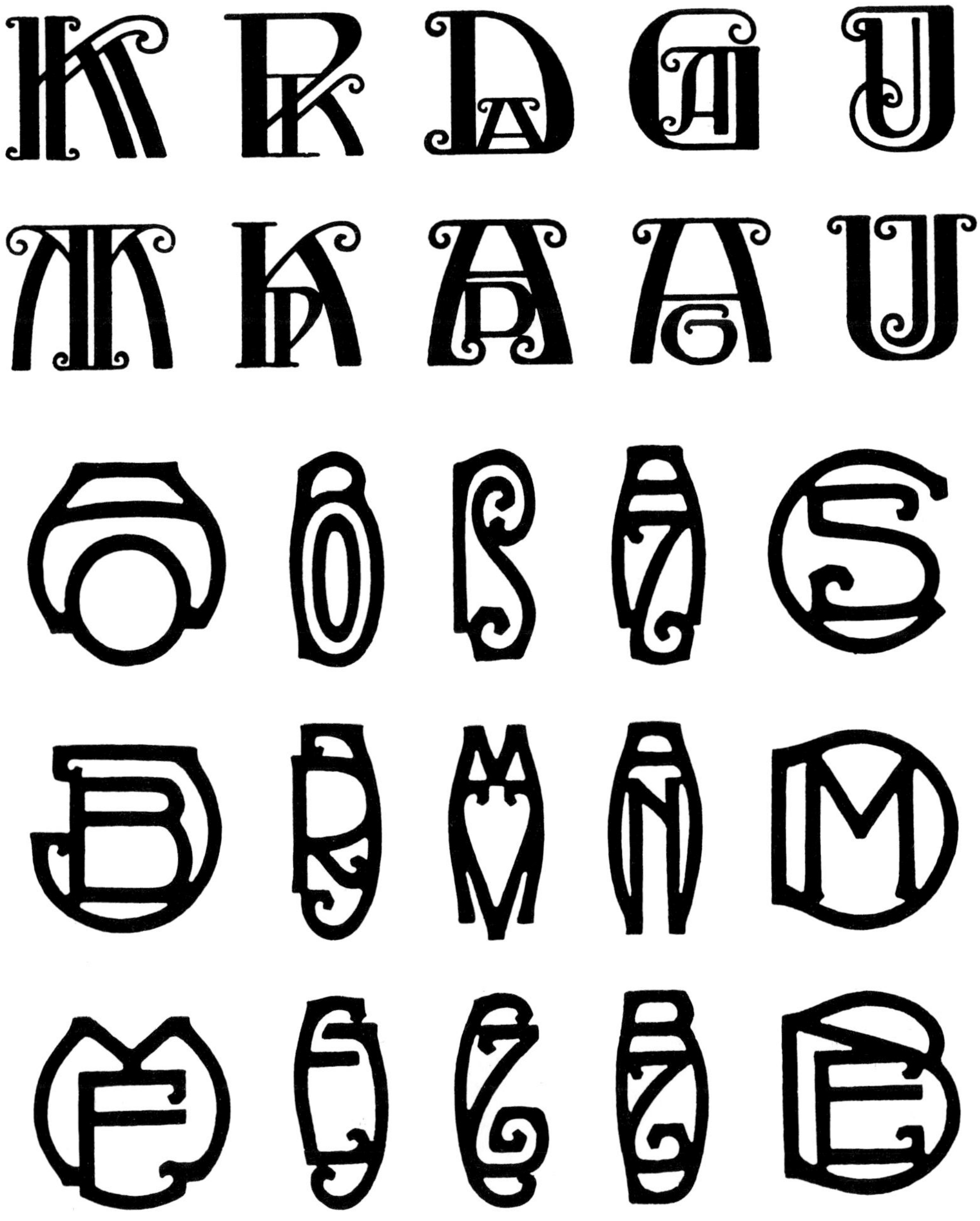

WT          MC          CA          VU          ON

HK          CL          QE          PJ          HA

EP          TC          KJ          QS

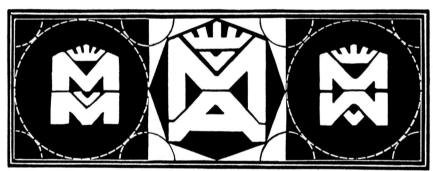

MvM          MvA          MvW

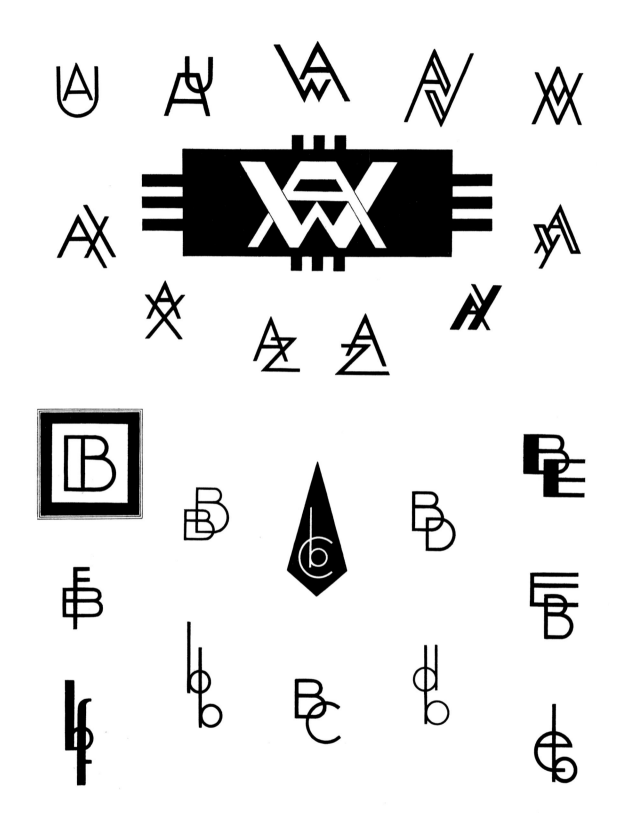

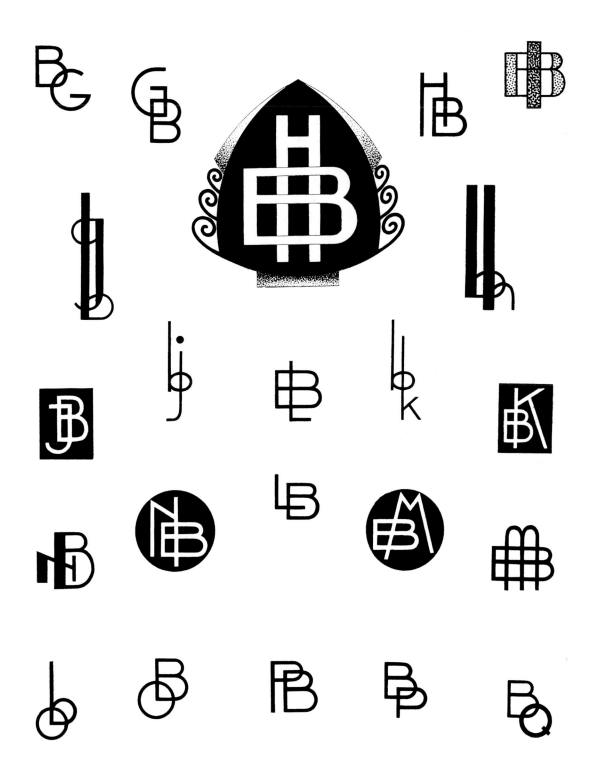

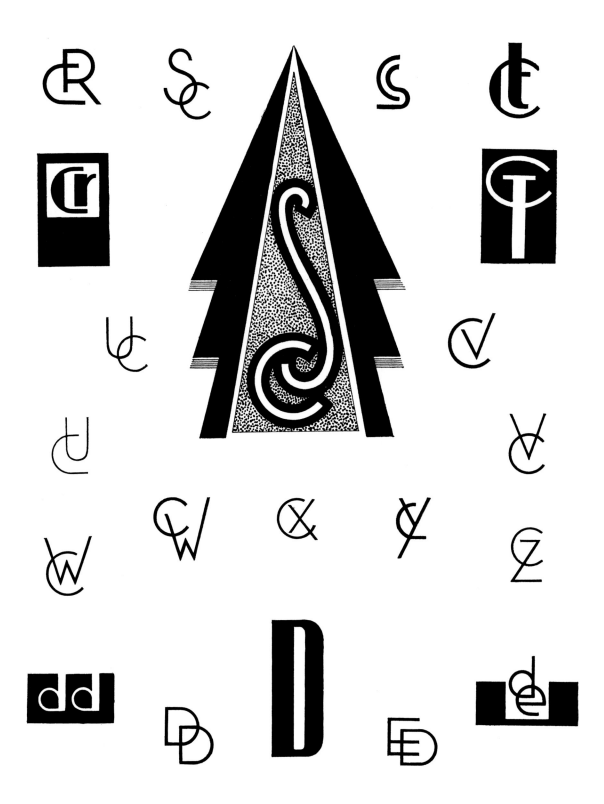

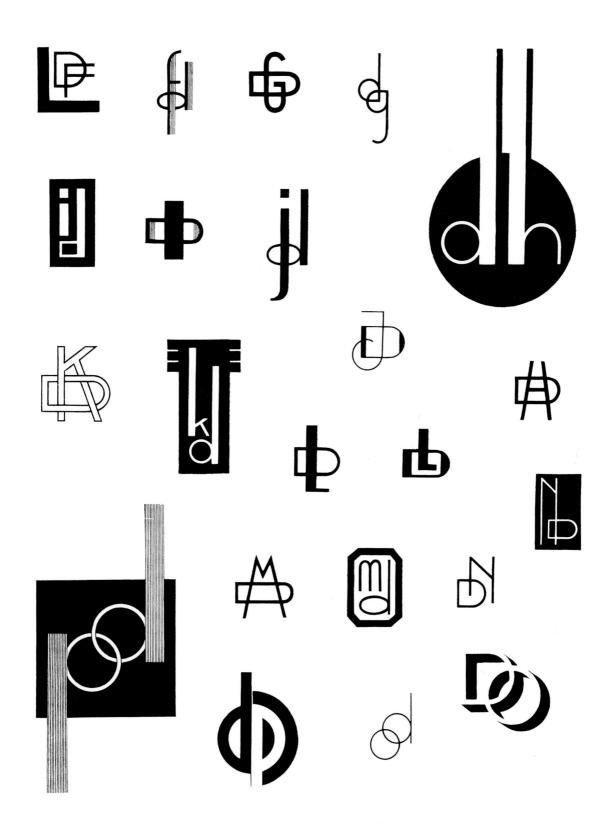

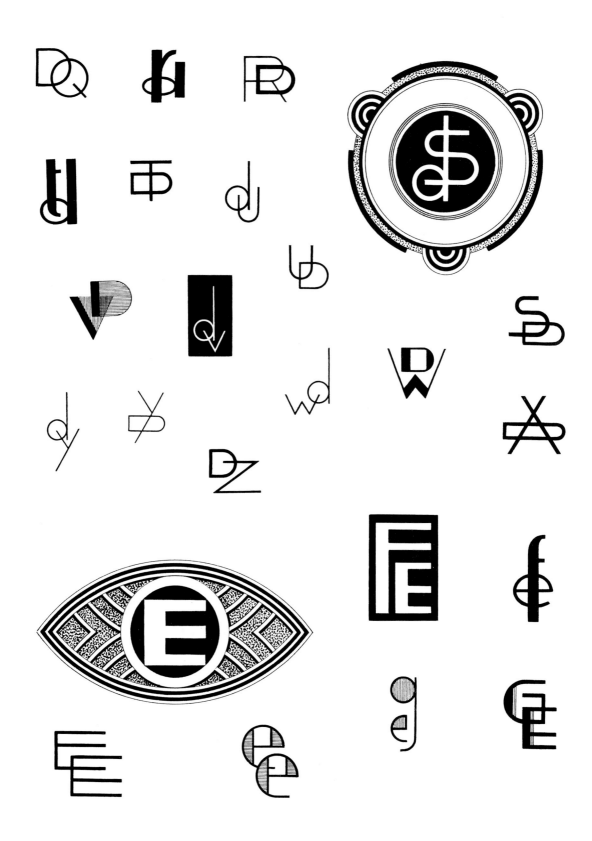

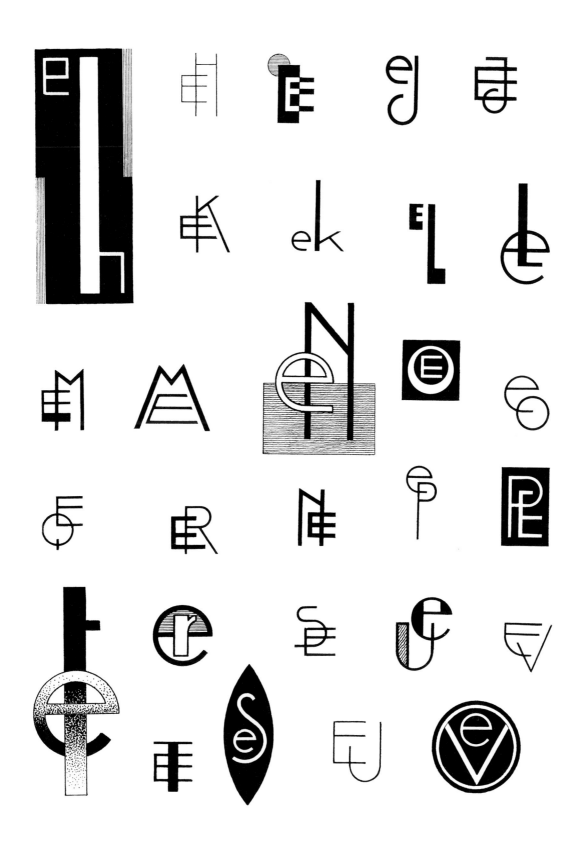

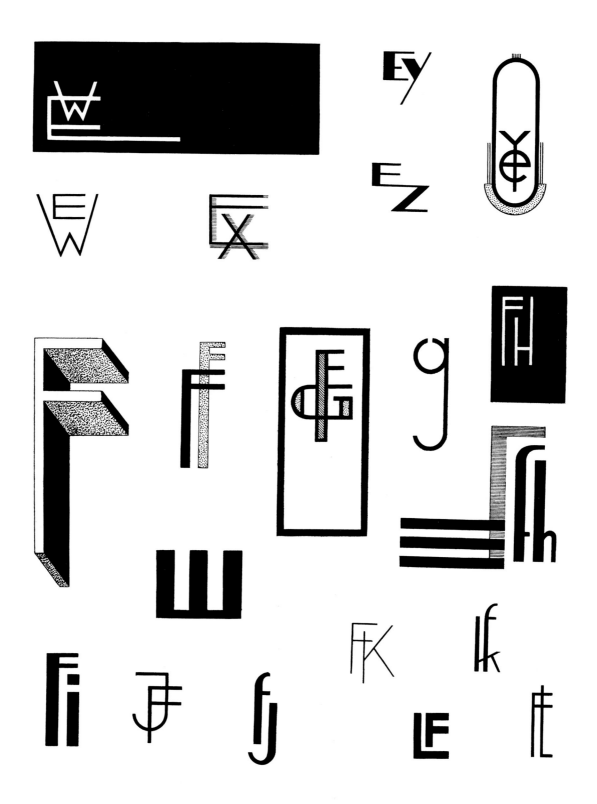

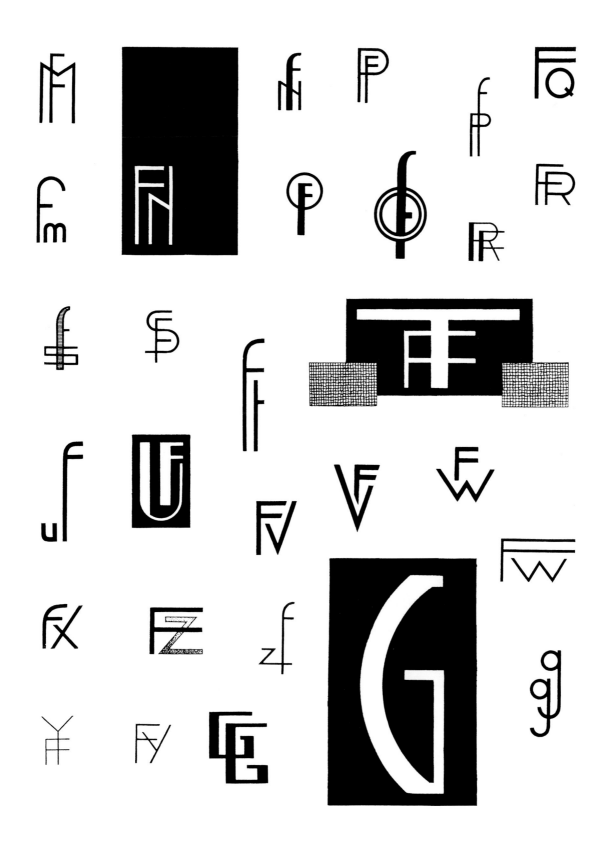

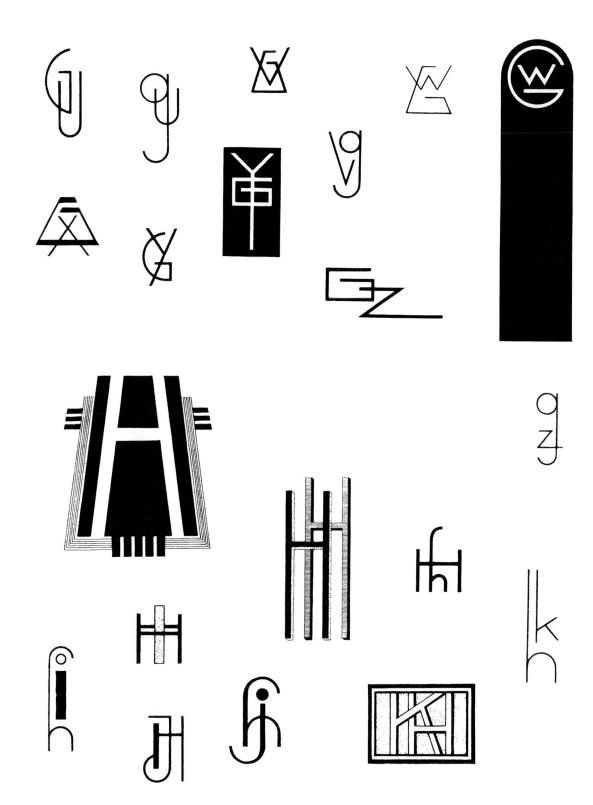

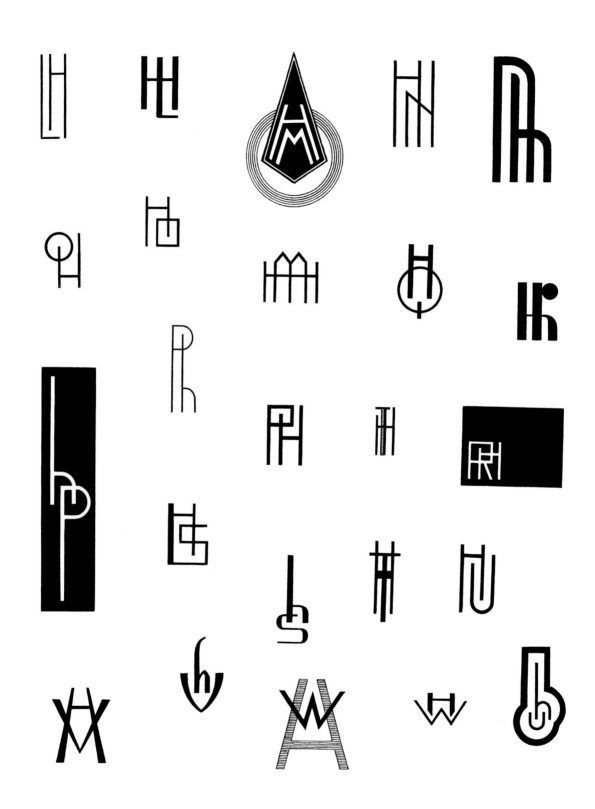

270

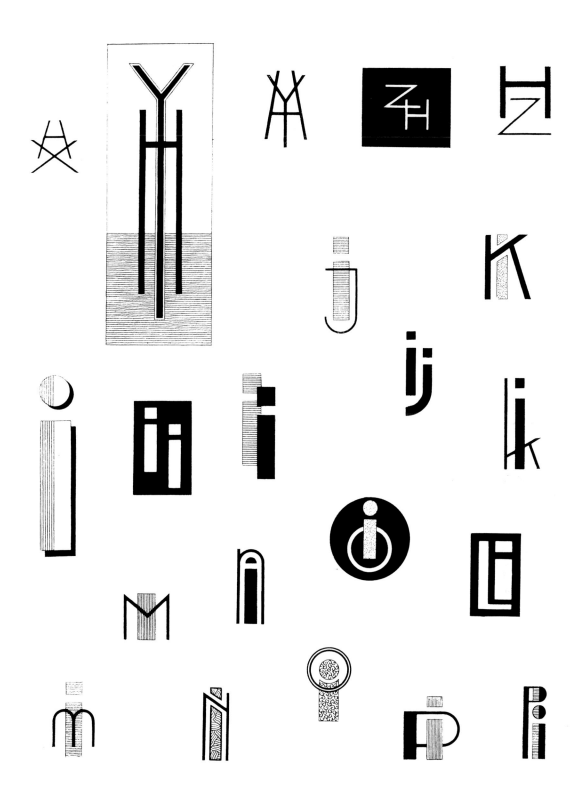

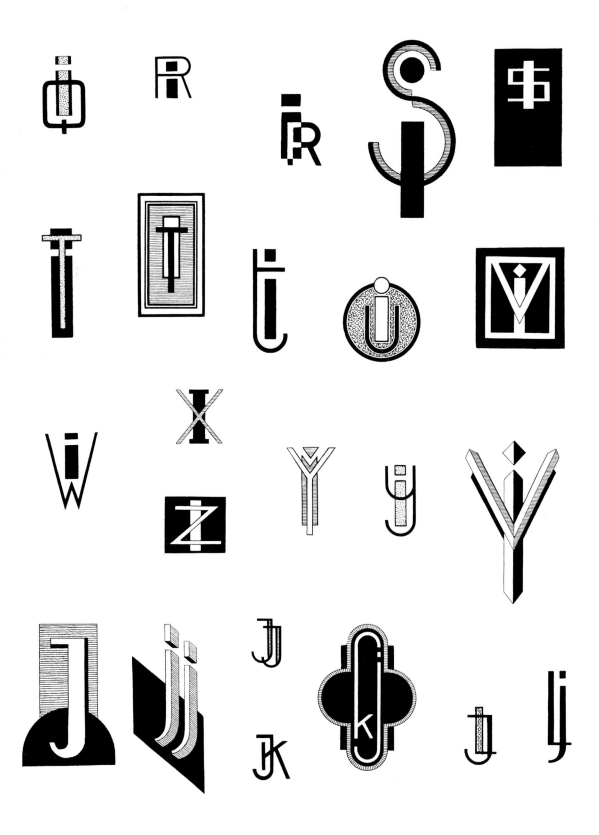

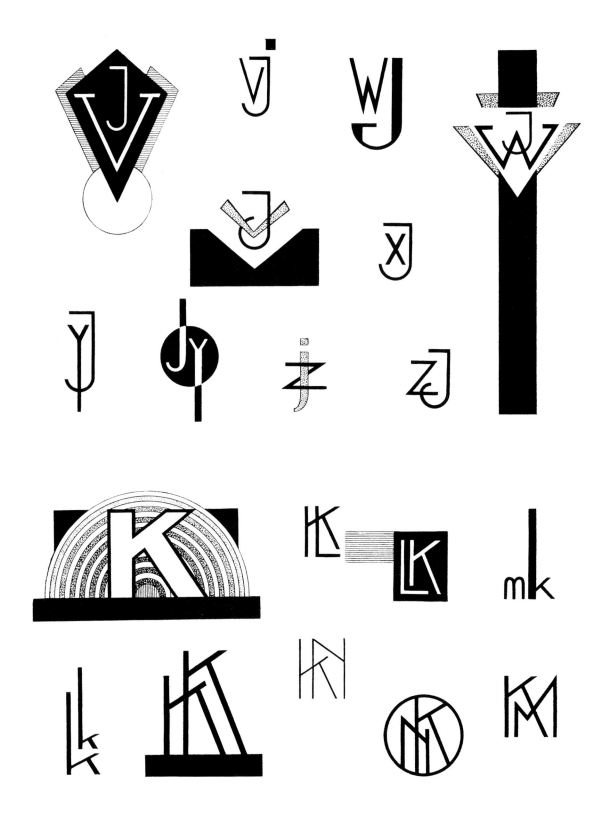

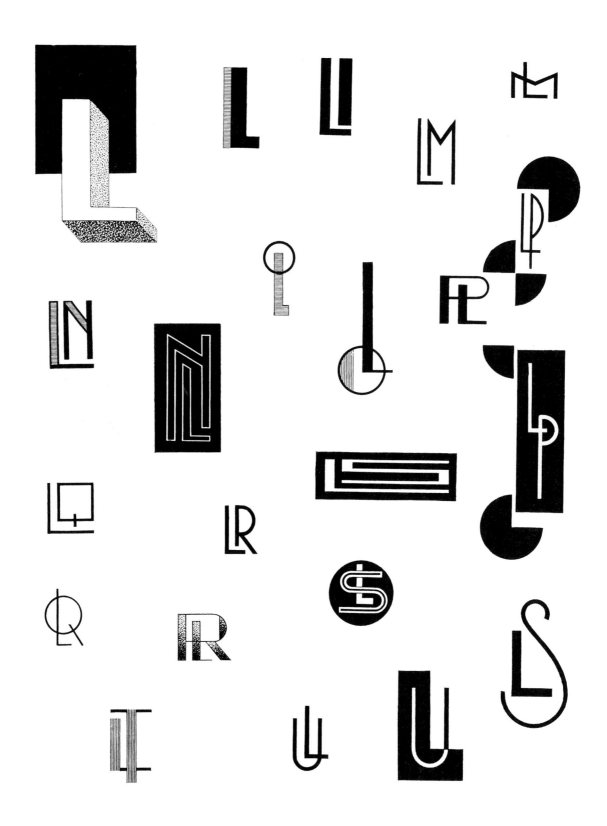

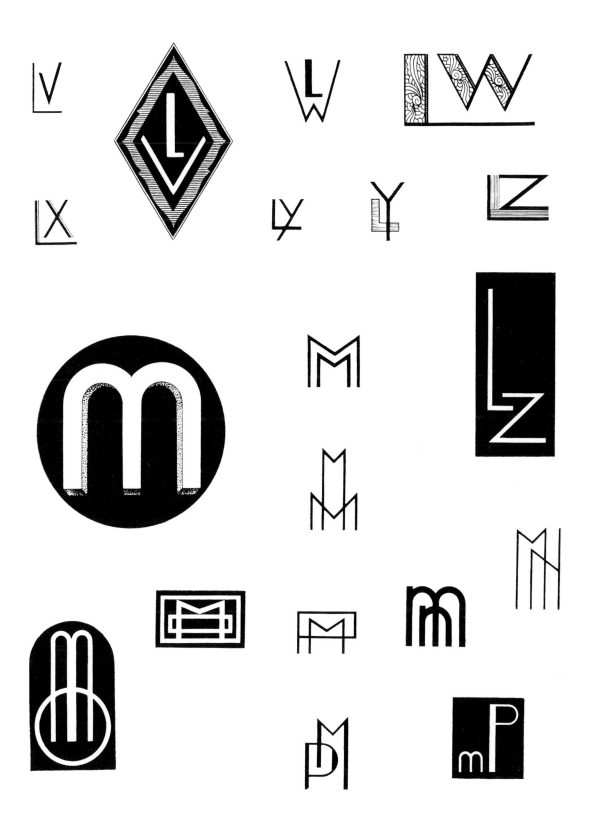

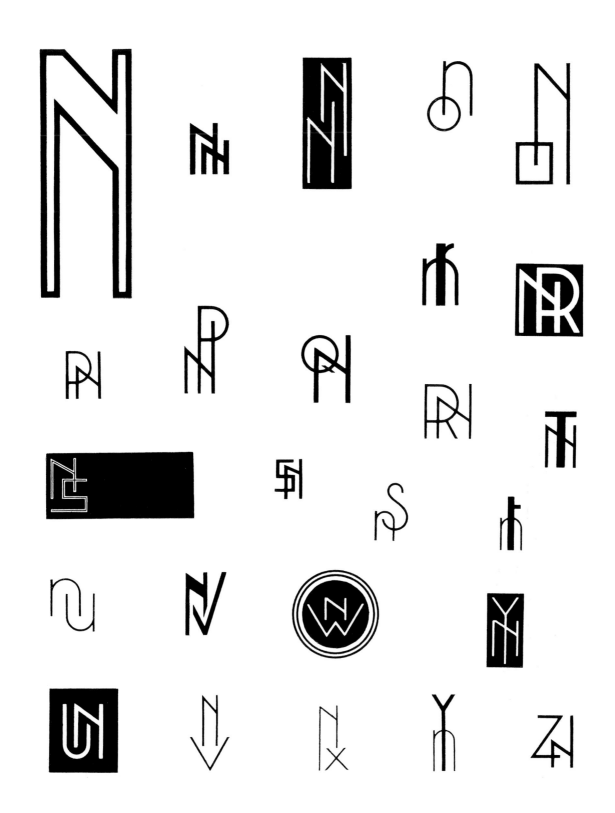

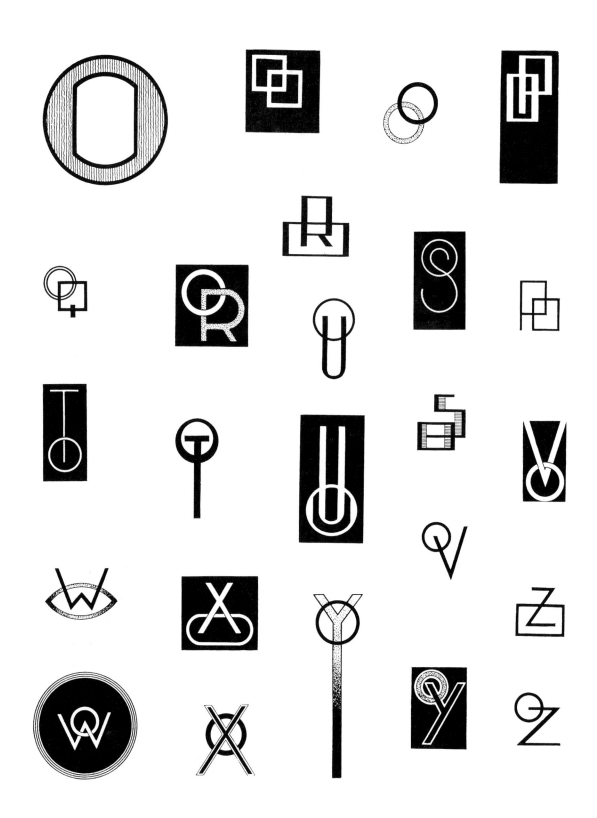

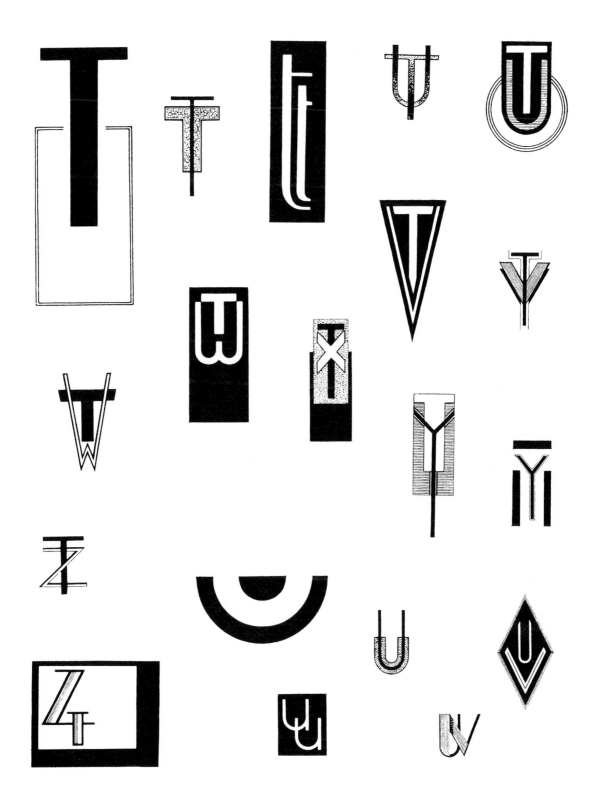

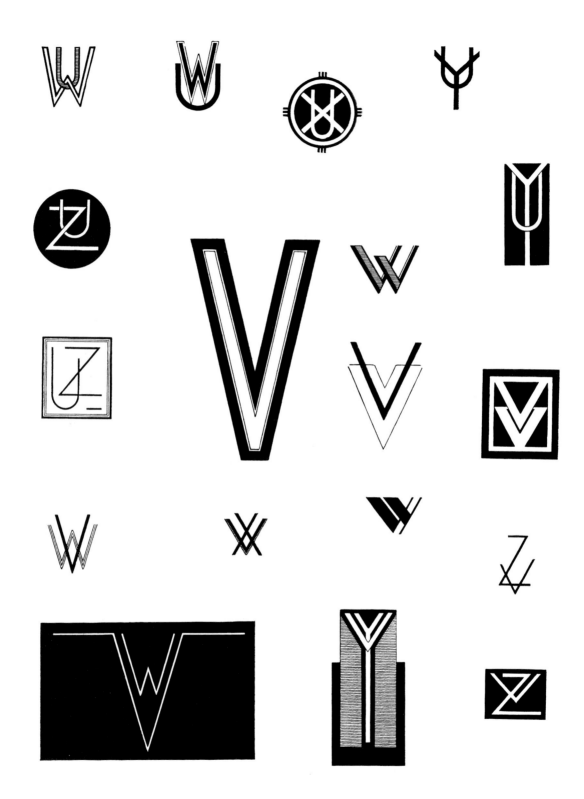

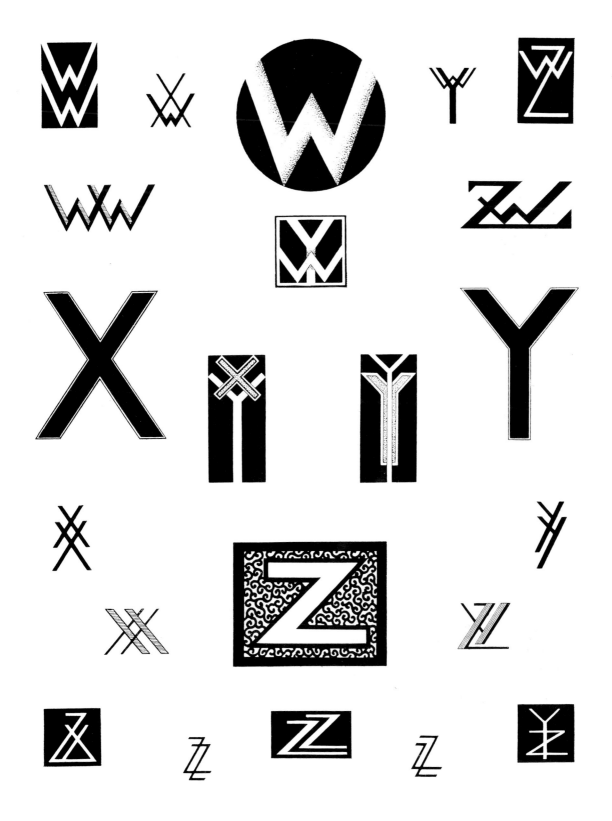